HE RESTORETH MY SOUL

ROZENA CAROLINE HORSLEY

ISBN 978-1-68526-436-9 (Paperback)
ISBN 979-8-88644-979-2 (Hardcover)
ISBN 978-1-68526-437-6 (Digital)

Copyright © 2022 Rozena Caroline Horsley
All rights reserved
First Edition

TXu 2-314-176.
This work is not an official publication of The Church of Jesus Christ of Latter Day Saints. The views expressed herein are the responsibility of the author and do not represent the position of the Church or of Covenant Books.

All rights reserved. No part of this publication may be reproduced, distributed, or transmitted in any form or by any means, including photocopying, recording, or other electronic or mechanical methods without the prior written permission of the publisher. For permission requests, solicit the publisher via the address below.

Covenant Books
11661 Hwy 707
Murrells Inlet, SC 29576
www.covenantbooks.com

A special thank you to Ammon Clanton for drawing the picture of Jesus Christ, that appears on the cover of the book.

The Lord is my shepherd
I shall not want
He maketh me to lie down in green pastures
He leadeth me beside the still waters
"He restoreth my soul"
He leads me in paths of righteousness for His name's sake
Yea, though I walk through the valley of the shadow of death
I will fear no evil
For thou art with me
Thy rod and thy staff they comfort me
Thou preparest a table for me in the presence of mine enemies
Thou anointest my head with oil
My cup runneth over
Surely goodness and mercy shall follow me
All the days of my life
And I will dwell in the house of the Lord
Forever and ever

—Psalm 23

He Restoreth My Soul

CHAPTER 1

The Beginning of My Life

I do not write the words of this book to have you think negatively about the people of my life whom I love with my heart and soul.

I must begin the story of my life at my age of eighty years and go back to the time I was an embryo. At the age of eighty, I received my DNA. I learned that I am 36 percent Scandinavian, English next, then Irish next. My parents and my only sibling are deceased and did not get their DNA prior to their departure. My physical appearance is quite different from my daddy, mother, and my sister. I was taught by my parents that their lineage is English, Irish, and Cherokee Indian.

In elementary school, I was forced by a few girls in my class to go into the girls' restroom at the school, and they washed my hair with soap and water to see if my hair was dyed. To their dismay, no color of dye appeared. My hair was auburn. My mother's hair was black, my daddy's hair was brunette, and my sister's hair was also brunette. I had some similar features. The girls teased me and told me I had to have been adopted. I asked my mother if I were adopted. Mother made it a point to prove I was not adopted.

Mother had me talk with Buela Miller (the wife and nurse of the doctor that delivered me in the home of my grandmother, Arnetta Rozena Powell). Buela Miller assured me that the day I was born, My heart was not allowing the necessary circulation in my body. She said that she and the doctor took turns massaging my heart from the morning of my birth throughout the night and until noon the next day to keep me alive.

This brings up the story that should explain: My parents, Violet and Paul, lived in Colorado, where Daddy had his own newspaper office. Daddy hired a man to come and work for him in his newspaper office. He was told that he could live with Daddy's family in a room in his home, as part of his wages. Mother and Daddy had a major quarrel. Mother left Daddy and took Peggy to Oklahoma. She was feeling ill when she arrived in Oklahoma and went to the doctor and learned that she was expecting a baby. She began smoking and drinking coffee, which she continued throughout the pregnancy. Could that be what caused the doctor and nurse to massage my heart when I was delivered.

Daddy learned about the pregnancy and left his business in Colorado to join Mother in Oklahoma. Mother and Daddy worked out their differences and never returned to Colorado. Daddy got a job working as a linotype operator for a newspaper office. Daddy loved Mother so much he was willing to forgive her and try to forget. Daddy would often sing the song to her "I'll Always Be in Love with You." He proved his love for her in so many ways.

Daddy agreed to sign his name on my birth certificate. Daddy was the best daddy I could ever have. He has been deceased since 1995. I look forward to the day I will be able to see him again and thank him for his love for me.

My sister evidently heard the arguing between Mother and Daddy. All through my growing up with her, she was very mean to me. Mother told me she had to watch her like a hawk around me. She would bite, scratch, and hit me when I was a baby. As we grew older, she constantly would say to me "He's my daddy."

When Daddy died at age ninety-five, my husband and I brought my mother into our home to care for her. She was eighty and lived with us for ten years prior to her death. Just before she died, she told me there was something she had to tell me. I waited, and she said nothing. I said to her, "Well, what do you have to tell me?" Tears came falling down her cheeks, and she said, "Rozena, I just can't tell you." It took me years to realize what she wanted to tell me. Now, I know. I was crushed for a time. Now, I completely forgive my mother for the past.

As I have thought about my life, the pain of memories as I was growing up and what I have learned about my DNA have helped me understand the story of my life. So now, my story begins.

CHAPTER 2

My Daddy

Memories of Daddy. He was such a good daddy—always concerned about me learning the true meaning of Christlike love for all people, integrity, kindness, and setting an example for me to follow.

Daddy talked about having a Christlike love for all people. A good example of this subject happened during a freezing ice storm. Daddy and I were down the street from our home. The power lines had so much weight from ice they were on the ground in some places. You can imagine how cold it was that day. A man was walking down the street and came close to us. He was wearing no coat. Daddy said "Hello" to him. Then Daddy took his coat off and gave it to that man. The man was so thankful. As Daddy and I walked back to our house, I asked Daddy, "Why did you give your coat away? You will freeze on our way home?"

Daddy answered, "I have a roof over my head to protect me from the storm. That man didn't even have a coat." What an example that Daddy showed me.

When I was two years of age, I was still sucking my two middle fingers with my forefinger and my pinky pointing up to my eyes. Daddy offered me $1 to stop sucking my fingers. I took the dollar. Later that day, I was sitting on the running board of the car, watching boys play football in a nearby field. Finger to fingers, I wasn't thinking about not sucking my fingers, and that's what I was doing. Daddy came around the car and saw me. He lovingly told me I had said I would no longer suck my fingers. He took the dollar back from me and explained that any time I gave my word for anything and took back my part of the bargain, it was wrong. I was to always keep my word, and that was so important. Through the years, he had other ways to teach me integrity. Those lessons have helped me so many times in my life.

Daddy had been told to never express his feelings of love for me through physical contact. That I was not to sit on his lap, kiss him on his cheek, or him kissing me on my cheek, and not express his feelings of love verbally to me. The only time he ever gave attention in that sort of way, he would put his arm around my shoulder and gently press the tips of his fingers into my arm. However, he would stand on his head and lean against the wall to make me laugh. I sometimes would see him coming home from work when I was very small and would run down the street and hold on to his little finger as we walked home together. As I grew older, he would be building onto our house, and he would ask me to be his gopher to hand him tools he needed.

We had a double corner lot. Daddy made certain that we had lots of flowers, chickens, ducks, gardens, trees, etc. Flowers: roses, petunias, iris, snap dragons, four-o'clocks, jonquils, and honeysuckle. Chickens: roosters, hens, baby chicks (it was my job to gather the eggs and be certain I didn't bring in the marked eggs that belonged to the setting hens…sometimes, I got pecked gathering the eggs. Ouch!).

Gardens: We had two nice-sized gardens. Yes, I got to help weed the gardens. We grew carrots, onions, okra, peas, green beans, etc. I enjoyed picking a carrot, washing it, and eating it as I walked to school. I sometimes gathered other vegetables and helped prepare them for dinner or canning. Trees: peach, plum, one small cherry tree, oak, maple, catalpa (which had long green beans, heart-shaped leaves, and flowers that would bloom a certain time of the year that eventually fell all over the yard and gave an appearance of snow). He climbed up that tree and installed a swing. He also planted mint by the faucets outside. We enjoyed asparagus as well as the fern from the asparagus to help decorate bouquets of flowers placed in a vase of water for the beauty and aroma in the house. We had milk and wine lilies that had a fragrance that completely filled an entire room. I thank Daddy for all he did for us.

When I was very small, I sometimes would awaken during the night because of extreme leg aches. I would cry. Daddy was always the one that came in to see what was wrong. I never asked or found out why he would rub turpentine on the bottom of my feet. (Perhaps it was a Kentucky remedy? He was from Kentucky.) He would rub my legs, and then he would place a penny in the palm of my hand, fold my fingers around the penny, and tell me to repeat over and over, "I believe in the power of the living God." I did that, and it helped to take my mind off the pain I felt in my legs.

An example of integrity and wisdom: When I was age five, we moved into a house known as the place we would not move from. It had one bedroom, where, of course, Mother and Daddy slept, and one living room, where a standard sized bed was where my sister and I slept. Peggy told me there was an imaginary line down the middle of bed. She warned that if I put even my little toe over that line to her side of the bed, she would beat me up. There was a porch that Daddy screened in. We had a kitchen. Oh yes, we had an outhouse. Daddy was thoughtful and bought (what we called) a honeypot so we wouldn't have to track through the snow or storms—which appeared often in Oklahoma—to go to the outhouse.

It took Daddy years to build another bedroom, an indoor bathroom, and a dining room with a fireplace. Three men came to our home to meet with Daddy. They had learned that Daddy owned a newspaper office in Colorado prior to him moving to Oklahoma. They asked him to print some graveyard ballots (that they would pay well for him to do). Daddy refused. It wasn't too many days later, a time bomb was placed in our car that exploded (thank goodness that nobody was in the car). Daddy thought they learned what time he left for work each morning because the time of the explosion was when he would have driven to work. I heard what the men were saying to Daddy, and when they left, I asked Daddy what graveyard ballots meant. He explained that they were ballots that had names of deceased people with their vote, which could help certain people win the election. After the explosion of our car, Daddy would not allow us to have a car again. And he stuck to that comment until Peggy and I were grown and away from home.

Daddy worked for a newspaper office in another town close to where we lived. He was the linotype operator. For years, he had to walk from our home to town and catch a ride to his employment, which was in another town. He always brought every dollar of his paycheck home to care for his family. However, he did buy marbles…one sack for Peggy, and one sack for me each payday. The boys in our neighborhood loved to come to our house to play marbles with me because they knew that when I would get the marbles, they would win them from me in no time at all.

I'll never forget Daddy bringing home $100 in cash, placing it on the table for us to see and telling us we were going on vacation. Aunt Vivian and Uncle Travis invited us to be guests in their home in Oklahoma City. We traveled to and from on a Greyhound bus. We went to Spring Lake Park. There was a swimming pool (that was something we sure didn't have in our town). Then we went to the zoo. The monkeys were so much fun to watch. Mother got too close to a big monkey, and he spit on her. She didn't think it was funny, but we enjoyed laughing. It was an unforgettable memory and such a thrill for each of us.

Once Daddy bought two bars of ivory soap. He gave one to me. We both sat down and carved that ivory soap. Daddy made a great dinosaur. I carved a crooked igloo. Daddy complemented my work. He also taught me to wrap gifts and print beautiful block letters.

Daddy was very good playing checkers. As a matter of fact, nobody I knew beat Daddy at the game. He taught me to play checkers. I never once beat Daddy. However, nobody could beat me after he taught me the game. It has been so many years since I have played checkers; I wonder if I could even beat someone these days.

He was the seventh son of ten children, plus two that died at birth. His dad was a Methodist minister and the editor and proprietor of the Harlan Enterprise that is still in existence today. When Daddy was a young boy, he would tell his parents he wasn't going to church. He was given a spanking and forced to attend church. Thus, when Mother went to church and took Peggy and me with her, as soon as we returned home from church, Daddy would be standing at our front door, ready to have contention in our home. Mother finally decided it would be best not to go to church. So we just quit going. I recall taking the Bible and reading the book of Job. I felt so badly for Job and the things he experienced. Another time, I read the entire book of Revelations. That frightened me so badly.

When Daddy was sixteen years of age, he lied about his age and joined the army during World War I. He didn't like to talk about his experiences in the army. However, one day, he had been lying down, with his shirt off on the couch, getting a treatment from an infrared lamp. When he got up, I could see deep scars on his chest and stomach area. I asked him what the scars were from. He told me that during World War I, he had been captured and managed to escape. He had to crawl for a long, long way. The scars were from having to stay on the ground to crawl so he wouldn't be seen and caught.

Another time, I went with him to the doctor. The walls were thin, and I could hear the conversation between Daddy and the doctor. The doctor had looked into Daddy's ear and asked him what had happened to him. Daddy told him that when he was captured during World War I, hot ashes had been poured down his ear. He wanted to know if the doctor had any medication that could help with the pain he was having. (The compensation Daddy received for the injuries he received during the war just couldn't cover the pain.) Daddy also served at Randolph Field, Texas, during World War II. Later in his life, he received recognition in newspapers and also was given a beautiful United States flag from the White House because of serving in World War I and World War II. Peggy was head librarian, and she sent the information about Daddy's military service to the White House. Thus, the flag was sent to Daddy with a letter of acknowledgment.

Daddy enjoyed playing games. Television was turned on to get the news, and then it was turned off. Games were actually helpful for our family to come closer together. There were board games and card games. When Peggy and I were adults and away from home, Daddy and Mother played games. There were card games such as pinochle, canasta, hearts, slapjack, etc. Board games such as monopoly, checkers, Chinese checkers, chess, clue, etc. Daddy always taught that if you play games, read, or write poetry, your mind will stay sharp. If you spend too much time watching television or listening to the radio, as you grow older, your mind will not function as well.

Daddy was example of this. He lived to be ninety-five years of age, and his mind was sharp. He never showed any signs of dementia or Alzheimer's all the way to departure from this earth. He was often referred to as a walking encyclopedia. By the way, along with playing games, he taught "no cheating." He also taught to play your best and compete with others and *always be happy when someone (other than yourself)* wins. He always taught if someone is known to be cheating, that was so wrong, and it was up to us to choose to be honest in all things. Integrity is up to us and to never follow a wrong example.

I was home in Nevada when a telephone call came from Mother. She called from Oklahoma. She told me Daddy had fallen, and she called a neighbor to help pick him up and put him to bed. I told her I would be on my way as quickly as I could get there. I lived in Overton, Nevada, and traveled to Las Vegas to catch a plane. Hartshorne has no airport, so I traveled to Oklahoma City. My cousin, Lee, and his wife, Wanda, met me at the airport. Lee had no idea that I didn't know Daddy had died. The first comment he made was, "I'm sorry you didn't get here in time to see your Dad before he passed away." He could have stabbed me through my heart, and it couldn't have hurt me anymore. I tried to get there so I could see Daddy. I know, he knew I tried. That did give me some comfort.

Daddy wrote poetry that was published in the World Poetry Anthology (editor and publisher was John Campbell). He wrote poetry until he died at age ninety-five.

At Daddy's graveside, he had military honors. There were trumpets playing taps, a six-gun salute, a United State flag on his casket, which was folded and given to Mother prior to lowering Daddy in the grave. Flowers were placed on the ground where he was buried. Family and friends were there to express their love and respect to Daddy.

I love my daddy!

CHAPTER 3

Mother

Mother was five feet tall and weighed ninety-eight pounds, soaking wet. Her skin was olive, her eyes were dark brown, and her hair was black. She was a pretty woman and lived to be ninety (not showing her age).

Mother, Violet, had a twin sister named Lilac. Mother never thought she was pretty. She was right. Mother was beautiful (inside and out). Whenever someone in the family was sick, she was the one that took care of them, no matter how difficult the task was. I was one that experienced her help. I witnessed her caring for her mother when she was suffering from cancer. She brought her mother into our home at my age of sixteen, and Mamama died when I was seventeen. During that year, Mother worked constantly to keep clothes and bedding clean. She cooked nourishing meals. She read to Mamama. She prayed for Mamama. Anything she could possibly do for Mamama, she did it without complaining.

The last surgery Mamama had, the doctors told Mother when they cut her opened that the doctor just had to stitch her back up. She had been treated with radiation and chemo, and everything had been done that could have been done for her. The end of her life, she was in a coma. The family took turns sitting by Mamama's bed to moisten her lips with water and being there if there was something they could do. Mother earned blessings from heaven for her efforts in caring for her mother. Also, for being there to help Aunt Lilac and Aunt Vivian (their sister, seven years older than the twins). That included traveling to wherever they were and being there to do all she could do. I even recall Mother caring for her grandfather as he was dying. To clean and feed him until his last breath. I was a very small child when he died. However, I remember it well.

I grew up in the house that my parents purchased. I recall each day someone would knock on our door. They were hungry and ask to be fed. Mother filled up a big plate of nourishing food and gave it to them. Never once did she refuse to feed them. I recall each evening after our family meal Mother making the comment "Our food has been blessed." This went on for years, and we never (not even once) went without food.

This brings up a memory. We had neighbors that would come to our home each day just before lunchtime—a woman and her two young boys. Mother would prepare lunch and asked them if they would have some lunch. The answer was always "Yes." This went on and on for a long time. Mother told Peggy and me we would not have lunch until they went home. (The thing I could see wrong with this is she should have fed us before they came over.) However, it was what it was. Sure enough, here they came…just before lunchtime. We visited…they stayed. After a while, I said, "I'm hungry." Mother looked at me as if she was warning me. More time went by. Again, I said, "I'm hungry." Again, I received a look of warning. Finally, they went home. I didn't get lunch quickly. Instead, I saw Mother pick up a yard stick. She lifted me on her bed and began to hit me with the stick. When I looked up at her, she had an expression that made me think she was going to kill me. I had never been so frightened. Well, the visits from our neighbors ceased. I learned a lesson I never forgot.

We had a neighbor that lived just across the street from our home. She was from Lithuania, named Bernice Drakis. She had an older husband, Frank, and they had two grown children, Walter and Amelia, who were living away from home. Bernice was quite the woman. She did all the chores. They had a cow, chickens, turkeys, and geese. She had a garden and went by the almanac to raise the most beautiful crop in town. She called her watermelon *wat-err-ma-lo-ne* with her accent. She told Mother she didn't believe in Christ.

She told about what she called the old county before she came to live in the US. She would go to church and confess her wrong doings and learned that she would be charged to pay for her sins. That did not go well with her.

One day, she came to visit with Mother and told her about Walter being drafted into the army. She listened on the radio and heard the area he was stationed had been bombed. She was wringing her hands as she told Mother that she prayed for Walter. Mother said to her, "Well, who did you pray to?" After that, Bernice did believe in Christ. I was home one day when her husband, Frank, came to our home and ask us if Bernice was there with us. We told him, "No." He said she never came into their house for a long time after she went out to do chores. Mother and I went to their place, walked out to their backyard, and found Bernice on the ground. She was dead. That was a shock that I have never forgotten. We loved Bernice. Amelia came home from Milwaukee and took her dad home with her. Their place was sold and the Drakis family was gone.

Before Bernice died, Mother would be cooking. She would sometimes be out of sugar or something she needed to prepare the food. She would ask me to take a cup and go across the street to see if Mrs. Drakis would lend her a cup of sugar, etc. (I would always go but would take a big stick if I needed to scare off her domestic turkey or geese. They were always trying to run up to me, and I felt the stick would defend me. It must have worked because I was never injured by them…just frightened.) As soon as Mother had sugar again, she would have me get a larger cup to pay back more sugar than she had borrowed. She also taught if I borrowed something from anybody, I was to pay it back *as soon as possible*, and if I borrowed something that I damaged, I was to repair it, and if I couldn't, I was to purchase a new one to replace it for the person from whom it was borrowed. This was another lesson I learned about integrity.

Mother and her twin, Aunt Lilac, were sixteen years of age when Mamama sent them to St. Louis Conservatory of Music in Missouri to study violin. After they were grown, they both taught music lessons to students. That included piano, violin, guitar, or accordion. Mother and Aunt Lilac played the piano and violin as well as sang at

Rotary, Kiwanis, Lion's, and church meetings. It was said that when they were so little, they had to be lifted on the piano bench to sing duets and play the piano. That made me believe they learned as spirits in a preexistence before coming to this earth. (The preexistence will be mentioned again within this book.)

Mother sewed. As Peggy and I were growing up, she made us dresses from feed sacks. They were beautiful. She was very talented with sewing. I recall once when we were in our teens, she made us floor-length gowns from crepe paper and bought us a mask that just covered our eyes. We looked royal to go to the town Halloween party, which was held in the gymnasium. She also made the same for Patsy, a neighborhood girl. Patsy was six years older than me and three years older than my sister, Peggy. Peggy and Patsy were close friends, and I was the tagalong.

Mother was taking charge of Mamama's café and Lee while Mamama was on a business trip. Mother talks about being busy during the lunch hour. From the corner of her eye, she saw Lee come into the café and take money from the cash register. She stopped him as he was hurrying out. She asked him what he took from the register. He lied to her and told her, "Nothing." She reached down in Lee's pocket and brought out a half dollar (Lee was in his early teens). Mother, as small as she was, took a brush, pulled down Lee's pants, put him over her lap in front of all the customers and began to spank him. She didn't stop until he cried. He was so embarrassed.

Later in Lee's life, he was in the military. Some of his friends decided to take a man's vehicle for fun during a furlough. They planned to get the vehicle back before the man got off work. As Lee was walking to join this group during their mischief, the memory of Mother spanking him came alive in his thoughts, and he wouldn't go through with their plan. The result of this story… Lee's friends went to prison for stealing a vehicle and were given a dishonorable discharge. Lee was safe.

Speaking of Lee, he was Aunt Vivian's child. When Lee was four years of age, Aunt Vivian asked Mamama if she would raise Lee (her grandchild). Mamama agreed. Mamama loved him so much. She nicked named him "IT." The story was told about Lee being on a hill above Mamama's café. He was playing marbles with some friends. Mamama wanted Lee to come to the café to eat lunch. She went to the back door of the café and yelled up at Lee. She said, "I...T," with her voice sounding as though she was singing "IT" with a high voice of "I" that lowered to the "T." He was so embarrassed. There were lots of stories about "IT."

Each Thanksgiving and Christmas, the entire family would go to Mamama's. She would close the café. There would be feast for the family to enjoy. After the delicious food, everyone would go up to Mamama's house, which was just a short walk up the sidewalk. Each member of the family would have a musical instrument such as piano, violins, guitars, ukuleles, and spoons. Lee always played an accordion or a harmonica and sang. He was really an entertainer, and everyone enjoyed his talent. Everyone would join in on a lot of the songs. That would go on for what seemed like hours.

There is a song titled, "Wind Beneath My Wings." When that song became popular, I used to sing it with thoughts of my mother. She played the piano for me to sing. She never expected any applause; she wanted me to shine. I performed many times and places as an amateur. I will write about this later in this book.

Even though Mother didn't say to me "I love you" or give me hugs or kisses on the cheek (which I needed so much), we had a good rapport with each other. One time, I was visiting between professional singing engagements, and Mother needed me to take her to get her a prescription. We had to sit in my car and wait for the prescription to be refilled. We had quite a wait and a bag of peanuts in the car and began to eat them. We took one peanut each and began slowly chewing. We agreed that as we ate the peanut, we would think about a pecan. We both agreed the peanut actually tasted like a pecan (the power of thinking). We repeated getting a peanut, and this time, we could imagine we were eating a cashew. We continued for a while with different kinds of nuts and then still had time left. We decided we would watch people go by and think what kind of dog each resembled. We laughed at how closely they looked like different breeds of dogs.

Mother told me when she turned sixty-five years old that she and her twin sister went to apply for social security. When Aunt Lilac went up for her interview and was asked her age, she told them, "I am sixty-five." They argued with her and didn't allow her to receive her social security because she had no birth certificate. When they asked her where she was born, she answered, "Little Onion Prairie, Oklahoma." She didn't know the actual name of where she was born, which is Blocker, Oklahoma—an unincorporated community located on State Highway 31 in Pittsburg County, Oklahoma, which was named for a local coal dealer named Blocker. The twins were born in their grandparents' home and never received a birth certificate. Aunt Lilac became irate and had to wait for her information to be checked out. Mother went up to apply for her social security. She was asked, "How old are you?" Mother answered, "I'm sixty-five." She was told, "You don't look sixty-five." Mother answered, "Well, my Daddy told me I am." She didn't have to wait to have the registration for her social security.

Mother truly loved Roy, my husband. When we telephoned and told Mother and Daddy we were driving to Oklahoma from Nevada to visit, she began making a devil's food chocolate cake. She made real fudge frosting from scratch. Within a very large oval-shaped baking dish, she put one layer of cake in the dish, frosted it, placed another layer of cake, and covered it with the real fudge frosting. When we arrived, Mother handed the entire cake to Roy. She said that the whole cake belonged to him. She told him it was okay to share it with everyone if he wanted to. (We all enjoyed the cake, and Roy felt very special.)

When Daddy died, we brought Mother to Nevada to live with us. She was eighty years of age and lived until she was ninety. She had a great sense of humor. One time, we had a box of cereal. On the cereal box, the words were "Fat free." Mother said, "Hum, they didn't charge anything for the fat."

Mother really liked Whitman's assorted chocolates. We always bought her a new box of chocolates whenever hers were gone. We decided to buy Mother a special box of See's chocolates for Christmas. She opened the package and asked where her Whitman's were? She didn't appreciate the change. So we bought her a new box of Whitman's assorted. I saw Roy coming out of Mother's room eating a chocolate as I was bringing her in the house in her wheelchair. I told Roy not to be going in to get Mother's chocolates. That was just for her. Mother corrected me. She said, "Roy can get my chocolates anytime he wants to."

As Mother advanced from eighty to ninety, she became progressively physically weaker. We took her with us on a family reunion. It was a beautiful area called Leman Cave. We had a comfortable place near a creek, with water running over the rocks and weather that was perfect for the occasion. She enjoyed herself so much. However, when we returned home, she had unusual coughing. She never wanted to go to a doctor. I told her, "Mother, I'm not asking you to go to the doctor. I'm telling you, you are going to the doctor." I called the doctor and made an appointment for her.

On the way to the doctor, she said, "Rozena, I want you to know I'm going to the doctor to please you. It's not for me. I don't want to go to the doctor."

I replied, "Thank you, Mother."

When we got to the doctor, he said to her, "Mrs. Eads, who is your doctor?"

She said to him, "My doctor died years ago."

He asked her, "Are you on any medication?"

She answered, "Yes, Epsom salts, castor oil, and whiskey."

The doctor asked, "Go easy on the Epsom salts, castor oil is good, and how much whiskey?"

She held up her thumb and forefinger and showed him about an inch as she explained, "That much every morning to jump start my heart." I could see the doctor biting his bottom lip to keep from laughing. The doctor wrote her a prescription. On the way home, I filled it and took her home. I didn't allow her to miss a dose, and she got well.

When Mother began thinking about the fact that she didn't have much longer to live, she began asking me questions about her burial. She wanted to know if she would be taken back to Oklahoma and being buried by Daddy. She asked about a casket, her burial clothes, etc. We assured her we will be flying her back to Oklahoma for her burial. I ordered a burial dress that was white with lace that she really liked. I asked her if she would like white slippers with lace to match her dress. She said, "No." She told me she wanted golden slippers. Her shoe size was 4 ½. It wasn't easy to find that size and color. I went to Las Vegas, Nevada, and found some pretty gold shoes and took them home for approval. She said, "No." I went back and found some pretty golden slippers, and they were the right size. I took them home, and she liked them.

I asked Mother, "Why do you want golden slippers?"

She said, "She was not going to die. She was going to twinkle." She wanted to be dressed appropriately. So she was almost ready. She wanted to purchase a gravestone for her and Daddy. She wanted their full names on the stone. It was easy for Daddy. However, she wanted her first, middle, maiden name, and married last name. When I ordered the stone, I was told it would be expensive. I told Mother, and she didn't care how much it cost; that's what she wanted. The stone was ordered, and the only thing that would have to be added would be her death date. She was satisfied and happy. So when the time came, everything to her liking was done. We knew she was accepting it all. One thing we didn't discuss with her was what I wanted. As she was buried, we had white balloons filled with helium and long streamers released. There were twelve balloons that we stood and watched as they flew away. I could imagine Mother up high gathering the balloons to give to the angels. There were beautiful flowers and special musical numbers. And, of course, family and friends gathered around to pay respects to Mother.

One day, toward the end of her life, I asked Mother, "What has been the greatest memory in your life?" I expected her to say "When I got married" or "When I gave birth to my first child." No, that was not her answer.

She said, "It was when you came by my house and took me with you to Carson City, Nevada. You were singing with Bob Wills. Bob Wills was called 'The King of Western Music,' and he was my hero. When Bob Wills learned that I play the piano and heard me play, he invited me to come on stage and join his band for a set. That thrilled me so very much. I shall never forget the happiness that brought."

I love my mother.

Paul and Violet Eads, Rozena's parents

CHAPTER 4

PEGGY

My sister, Peggy, lacked eighteen days being three years of age when I was born. Mother told me she had to watch Peggy like a hawk because she would bite, scratch, pinch, or hit me. As I grew, her attitude toward me did not change. Mother told me when I got old enough and tried to play with Peggy's toys, Peggy got a box and filled it with her toys, took it to the front yard, and gave her toys away to children as they passed by. Mother said when she asked Peggy why she gave her toys away, Peggy said, "So Rozena can't play with them."

    Mother taught music lessons (piano, guitar, and violin) in our home. Peggy was free to do whatever she wanted against me. She got me down and tickled me to make me laugh. Only problem, she wouldn't stop. She tickled me till my laughter changed to tears. She did this to me day after day. Could it be that Mother couldn't hear what was going on because of the noise the music lessons? Somehow, I managed to make up my mind that I would not be ticklish. It took a lot of deep concentration. Perhaps hearing the music as Mother taught her students helped me to succeed. Well, that did the trick! When Peggy got me down and tickled me, I didn't laugh, nor did I cry. She no more had fun with the tickle torment.

    I don't know where she came up with her ideas. Her next torture was to hold me against a wall with one hand and with her other hand point her finger very close to my face between my eyes without touching me with her pointed finger. She wouldn't let me go until I cried. At least, that was short lived. Peggy was much bigger, heavier, and stronger than me. That's why I couldn't fight back, plus, nobody was teaching me to defend myself or bothering to discipline Peggy.

It was a hot day. Humidity in Oklahoma caused misery to a body in very hot weather. Peggy suggested, "Rozena, let's put on our swimsuits and run through a sprinkler attached to the hose in our yard." It felt so good to have that cool water ease the heat of the sunshine. Suddenly, I felt the blow of Peggy hitting me so hard on my back that it knocked the breath out of me. It seemed like it took forever to be able to breathe again. As soon as I could breathe, she hit me again. I must have turned mighty pale because after the second blow, she didn't hit me again. I cannot even remember why Mother said nothing about the mark on my back. It had to be impossible to see that I had been abused.

One day, Peggy told me we were going to play with Patsy. Patsy was three years older than Peggy. Of course, that made her six years older than me. I was so excited to even have Peggy act as though she liked me and wanted me to go someplace with her. When we arrived at Patsy's house, they had a plan. Peggy said, "Rozena, we're going to put up a ladder and climb up to the hay loft and play games. I was afraid to climb the ladder because of the height. Patsy said, "Rozena, don't be a baby. You go up first, and I'll be right behind you and won't let you fall. Peggy will be behind me…so go!"

I climbed the ladder and managed to get on the loft. They hurried down the ladder and then took the ladder down. There I was… all alone on the hay loft. I begged them to get me down. They just laughed at me and disappeared. I was on that loft all day—no food, no water, but lots of tears. It was almost dark when they returned. All they did to help me down was put the ladder back so I could climb down. When I looked down, I was so scared. I sure didn't want to spend another second up there alone, so I managed to climb down.

Patsy told Peggy, "We have to call your mother and tell her I have to stay all night by myself and I'm scared. My Aunt Sugar wants me to stay in our home, and I really need you to stay with me. We can't let your mother see Rozena with red swollen eyes, or we will get in trouble. So it was no problem at all to have Mother agree we could stay overnight with Patsy. There is more to the story."

Patsy and Peggy had some cigarettes. They smoked them. Patsy told Peggy, "We have to force Rozena to smoke a cigarette, or she will tell on us." They told me to suck on the cigarette and take a deep breath, then swallow the smoke. I choked, and it hurt me. I was so sick. The next morning, it was time to go home. Patsy and Peggy threatened me that I would be beaten up if I told Mother what they had done to me.

Well, this time Patsy came to our house to play. What a game they told me we were going to play! Patsy said, "I'm the queen."

Peggy said, "I'm the Princess."

Peggy said to me, "Rozena, you are our slave or you can't play."

Immediately, Patsy said, "Rozena, go in the house and make us some peanut butter and crackers, put them on a tray, and when you bring them to us, bow and say, here is your lunch, your majesty. Then serve them to us. Now, go and pick some heart-shaped leaves from the catalpa tree and fan us and keep us cool." Why didn't I just walk away? I wanted the company so I wouldn't be all by myself.

We had a playhouse in the backyard. Peggy, Patsy, and I were in the playhouse. Mother had a break from giving music lessons and brought three big pieces of watermelon for us. As soon as she went back into the house, Patsy said, "Peggy, let's tie Rozena to the pole in the middle of the playhouse and eat her watermelon."

Peggy laughed and immediately grabbed me. They put me against the pole, stretched my arms behind me around the pole, and tied my hands so I couldn't get away. They ate my watermelon in front of me, put the rind on top of my head, and danced around me, squeezing the watermelon seeds between their thumb and finger, trying to make them stick on my face. Oh yes, I cried. That made them happy to see me cry and called me baby.

One Saturday, Mother gave Peggy a quarter and told her that would pay for her and Rozena to get in to the movie. There would be a nickel left, and she could buy a sack of popcorn and share it with me during the movie. When we got to our seats, she began to eat the popcorn. I reached over to get some popcorn and took a few pieces.

She slapped my hand and said, "Eat one piece of popcorn at a time and eat slow." She took a handful of popcorn, and the popcorn was gone very quickly.

More than once, Peggy walked me to town to get an ice cream cone for each of us. Peggy ate her ice cream fast and took mine away from me and ate every bite of what I had left.

When we were in our teens, Mother said, "Rozena will you walk to town and find Peggy? Tell her to come home right away because I need her." I went to a place called The Pine Tree, which was a place the teenagers hung out together. Peggy was sitting at a booth with other teenagers. She was smoking a cigar.

I went over to her and said, "Peggy, Mother asked me to find you and tell you she needs you and to come home right away." Peggy looked up at me, got up and slapped me on my face really hard, and sat back down. She refused to go home. Oh yes, I was hurt and so embarrassed.

One day, I was writing in my journal. Peggy came in and grabbed my journal and said, "Ha, ha, I'm going to read your journal. She ran through the room where Mother was giving a piano lesson. I ran after her, and I pushed her down, which certainly disturbed the piano lesson. I got my journal back, and Peggy cried. Her arm was hurt. Frankly, I didn't care.

Peggy and I actually became "sisters" after Mother died. Peggy would call me on the telephone, and we had good conversations about how she was doing, and she wanted to know how I was.

I am so grateful for that change in our relationship. She died August 20, 2009, at the age of seventy-two. I'm so happy that I wrote her a letter and told her, "Please forgive me for anything I have ever said or done to hurt you in any way. I want you to know I forgive you for anything you have ever said or done to hurt me." If I hadn't sent that letter, it would be so difficult to have her on the other side and me on this earth without her.

I love Peggy.

Peggy Jean Eads-Suter, Rozena's sister

CHAPTER 5

Rozena's Experiences

When I was two years of age, Mother taught me the words to a hymn, "Trust and Obey." The lyrics that I remember were:

> When we walk with the Lord, in the light of His word,
> What a glory He sheds on our way.
>
> When we do His good will, He abides with us still.
> And with all those who Trust and Obey
>
> Trust and Obey, for there's no other way
> To be happy with Jesus, but to trust and obey.

In a Baptist church meeting, Mother accompanied me on the piano as I sang "Trust and Obey" as a solo at the age of two.

One day, I was with Mother as she worked in her mother's (Mamama's) café. There were many customers there for lunch. I had a little child's toy broom with straw that was made just like an adult's broom. There was an open face stove that was lighted to keep the café warm. I stuck my broom into the fire. Of course, the straw caught fire very quickly. I was frightened. I began going around and around, still holding the broom. This caused the fire to get bigger. There was a customer who managed to quickly get right behind me, grab the broom, and take it immediately outside, where he put out the fire. I have a clear and distinct memory of this incident.

Mamama had a nickelodeon in her café. When the music was playing, I would dance to entertain the customers. Nobody asked me to dance, and I had never had dancing lessons. I could feel the rhythm of the music, so I moved my little feet as I enjoyed the songs that were played. The customers would actually give me coins to have me keep dancing.

When I was eight years of age, Mother accompanied me on the piano as I sang the song "The Band Played On" over a KNED Radio Show in McAlester, Oklahoma.

The lyrics were:

> Casey would waltz with a strawberry blonde.
> And the band played on.
> He waltzed ore' the floor with the girl he adored.
> And the band played on.
> His heart was so loaded it nearly exploded.
> The poor girl would shake with alarm.
> He married the girl with the strawberry curls.
> And the band played on.

Mother told the story about when I sang ("The Band Played On"), I held the word *played* a very long time, such as "And the band p…l…a…y…e…d o…n." I guess that's the way I felt it.

For years, I didn't continue to sing (except for myself.) Now, I was fourteen years of age. A big Halloween party was held in the town's gym. There was an advertisement that there would be a talent contest held during the Halloween party. Mother and Peggy told me I should sign up for the talent show. I told them, "Absolutely no."

They continued to tell me, "Rozena, sign up." This went on so long that I did sign up for the talent show just to get them to quit harassing me.

Again, Mother accompanied me on the piano. I sang "I'd Rather Die Young." When I walked up to the microphone to sing, I looked out at the crowd of people and butterflies began to have the opportunity to fly around inside my tummy (at least that's how I felt). However, there I was with only one way out. That was…*sing!* I was so frightened I could feel my knees shake. My teeth felt like they were hitting against my other teeth between breaths as I sang the words.

Finally, I somehow got through the song. I took my place on the bleachers to enjoy the other contestants. The announcer came to the microphone. He announced the winner of the third place. Then he announced the winner of the second place. Then he announced the winner of the first place. You could have knocked me over with a feather as I heard him announce my name: "Rozena."

He called me back to the stage and handed me a $25 savings bond and announced that I also won an automatic entry for another talent show that would be held in a town nearby the following week. So I was committed to sing again! I won second place in that event.

That was the beginning of me being an amateur entertainer and being asked to sing in many places. I sang on TV Shows in Ada, Oklahoma City (a guest for Hank Thompson's show), and Tulsa, Oklahoma. I was asked to sing at civil organizations such as Rotary, Kiawana, Elks, etc.

I was asked to travel on a state-wide tour to advertise the prison rodeo, which was held in McAlester, Oklahoma. There were several other singers that traveled with that tour. Oh, what an experience that was. It was mandatory that my parents went with me inside the state prison to rehearse with the prison band. As we walked through the prison, I could see inmates wearing their striped clothes and locked up in their cells. That was frightening to me. The inmates were standing at the bars, looking at us walk by.

We were protected by armed guards, and they led us to the room where the prison band was waiting for us to rehearse. There were armed guards all around that room. The members of the band were very talented. It was so easy to sing with them accompanying me. To listen to the music they played was very uplifting.

In that rehearsal room, there was a musician that talked to me. He told me whenever I got a chance to go to Dallas, Texas, to go to the KRLD-TV Studio and tell the receptionist at the front desk you want to audition for John Hitt. I was to tell her the name of the man that told me to ask for the audition, however, not to tell anybody he was serving time in prison. I was fourteen years old when I was instructed to go to Dallas, Texas, and I was eighteen before I actually went. I will explain more about this story later in this book.

Meanwhile, we're going back to when I was six years old, and school started for me. I was so excited. In my hometown, they didn't have kindergarten. Instead, they started the first year calling it primary. Any student had one half year to be in primary, and if they performed well, they would be advanced to first grade for the remainder of the year. Others remained in primary until the end of the school year. They would return the next year as first graders if they performed well.

I learned quickly to count to one hundred. I could also write from one to one hundred. My teacher's name was Mrs. Park. I asked her if I could stay in the classroom during recess and write from one to one hundred on the black board. She gave me a positive answer. I was so happy to have my desire granted. I wonder if the other students thought I was being punished because I remained in the classroom and wrote from one to one hundred on the chalkboard. I didn't care what they thought. The thrill was mine.

I recall going to music class in first grade. The teacher, Mrs. Carmel Johnson, called the roll. Her method was, if she were calling my name, she sang, "Rozena, I am calling. Rozena, where are you now?"

I was taught to sing my answer. I sang one high note "I'm," then I sang the low note "here." Singing "I'm here," I had to sing a perfect octave. I had no problem doing that. I felt sorry for those that couldn't sing an octave. We were graded on our two octave notes.

Mrs. Johnson was amazing. Our music class began going down to the basement of the school about one month prior to the first day of May. There was a maypole with streamers and a piano in the room. We were each taught to pick up a streamer, and we were placed around the maypole as girl-boy, girl-boy, etc. We were taught to dance around the maypole by the left foot being lifted to the right knee followed by the right foot being lifted to the left knee. We were taught to form a pattern with the streamers such as "a spiderweb," etc. We were taught a few patterns. There was a song which was played on the piano which gave us a hint which pattern we were making.

We were also taught the streamers were to be lifted over the head of our partner and continue to lift our streamer over others until we met our partner again and knew to stop with our partner. We then would begin to form our next pattern. It didn't take long to learn what we were doing. When we went to the high school football field to perform our maypole, there were six maypoles on the field, three on each side. There was one maypole for each grade (one through six). Mrs. Johnson, a perfectionist, required that girls wore the same color dresses which matched the color of the boy's ties. Each class (first grade through sixth grade) had a different color assigned for their girl's dresses and boy's ties.

The bleachers were where the parents sat to observe the May Day show. They were able to see the different patterns at the end of each song. The streamers were held high by the children performing at the end of each maypole dance.

My best friend, Annette, and I were chosen to be the majorettes. Our first-grade majorette outfits were identical to the high school majorette's outfits. As we marched out onto the field with our batons, I felt chills because I was so excited. There were speakers placed on the poles of the football field which played patriotic music for our first-grade band to make the grand entry of the occasion. Our entire first-grade band marched behind Annette and me. They played bird whistles, bells, drums, a cymbal, triangles, etc. Of course, the patriotic music coming through the speakers were playing along with the first-grade band.

We had a place to get dressed to go to our first-grade maypole and take part in the maypole show. More about Annette…

I will always remember Annette and I having one very big lollipop that we sat outside on the school ground during recess. Annette would lick on one side of the lollipop, and I licked on the other.

We both had a crush on a boy in our class. His name was Rudy. We would argue about which one of us was his girlfriend. The stress between us ended when Rudy moved away from our town.

The elementary school was called "North Ward" and the junior high through high school was across town and called "South Ward." When high school began for me, I was chosen to sing contralto in the High School Trio, the High School Quartet, Mixed Chorus, Girl's Glee Club, etc. Our school's music department traveled to other schools across the state to compete in contests held in different places. We were judged as superior-plus performances most of the time. I contribute that to having Mrs. Carmel Johnson for our teacher.

One day, the entire high school was meeting in the auditorium. Our high school trio was singing "Ole King Cole." Our soprano, Carolyn Jo, had a solo part in the song. She sang "Fiddle Diddle Dee Went the Fiddle;" our second soprano's solo part was "Fiddle Diddle Dee Went the Drum;" I sang contralto, and my solo was "Fiddle Diddle Dee Went the Big Burley Bumbo, Fiddle Diddle Diddle Diddle Dee."

As I sang my solo part, the arrangement became slower and slower and slower. Then the words of the song became lower and lower and lower. Our trio was seeing all the students as they listened to the end of the song, and their eyes grew bigger, and their heads were lowered as they heard the lower notes being sung. We began to laugh, and then we couldn't control our laughter. When the assembly was over and we returned to the music room, Mrs. Johnson was there. She refused to say a word to us. Not just that moment, but the silence treatment to us continued for days. We felt so badly that she was so upset with us.

I was a junior in high school when Mrs. Johnson had our music department present a Christmas Candlelight Program for the entire town to attend. The lights were lowered, and each one that sang in the music department wore the graduation robes and entered in the front of the building. Each student held a lighted candle as we marched slowly in while we hummed the hymn "Come All Ye Faithful." There were candelabras set up for each of us to place our lighted candle prior to singing the beautiful Christmas hymns. I also played the timpani drums during the program. I sang a solo "Sweet Little Jesus Boy." It brought tears to my eyes. I am so grateful for the opportunity to have been a part of that program, plus all the other memories I have of knowing Mrs. Carmel Johnson since I was in the first grade of school.

I had no thought of running for president of my sophomore year in high school. I had friends who urged me to do just that. They made posters for me for the advertisement that I was in competition. Again, you could knock me over with a feather when I realized I won the campaign. That was a good experience. There was a student that truly had a problem, and I was concerned about it. The girl was born with a double hair lip, and her family didn't have the money for surgery. She tried to talk, and nobody could understand what she was saying. Another girl tormented this sad student. There was no mercy for her.

I called for an assembly. I got up and didn't mention names. However, I gave a talk about the importance of being kind to others. I heard that the girl that was tormenting the student to be so sad later in life was married and had three children. I was told her three children were all born with a double hair lip, and they all required surgery. What a sad story. The principle of karma teaches "Cast your bread upon the water, and it will return to you tenfold." That is whether it is good that you do or bad that you do. Hopefully, anyone that reads this book will think twice before they are unkind to others.

Another story that I'd like to share with others is about learning to whistle. The boys in my neighborhood could whistle very loudly without using their fingers to whistle. I was so impressed and wanted to whistle the same as the boys. I tried and tried and tried. Actually, it was over a year that I failed to whistle. I wouldn't give up. Each day, I spent many times trying to whistle with no success. One day, I was riding my bicycle while I tried to whistle. I surprised myself when I did it! I whistled! I didn't use my fingers in any way. From that day on, I not only whistled without my fingers' help; I whistle very loud!

If you don't succeed the first time, try…try…again!

CHAPTER 6

JESUS CHRIST IS MY BEST FRIEND

I am never alone. My best friend of my entire life is Jesus Christ. I can talk with Him, walk with Him, turn to Him, draw close to Him, smile with Him, feel His love for me, and show my love for Him by doing my best to keep His commandments. And when I sometimes say or do things that I know isn't right, I repent with a broken heart and a contrite spirit. That causes me to cry and say a very long prayer as I think of my Savior. I know that He knows I am truly sincere.

What a blessing!

Though I have experienced deep hurt from the time I entered this earth life, I have also felt the love of my Savior. Oh, I have been depressed many times. However, I have loved those who hurt me. I am so happy that has been the case. I have always wanted to live my life doing the will of my Savior. Even though at times I have had problems with sin. I have repented to people I have offended, with deep sorrow within my heart, and then go to my Savior in prayer and repented to Him. I feel the forgiveness enter into my soul.

I had a dream about Jesus Christ when I was very young. I recall that dream often. I was standing in front of a large white building. There was a forceful wind. It was a sandstorm. I looked down the street and saw a man wearing a white robe and holding His hand over His eyes to protect His face from the sand that was blowing. He walked up to the front of the building where I was standing and walked up the many stairs. He came and stood in front of me. When

He lowered His arm, I could see that it was Jesus Christ. I knew Him because of the many pictures I had seen of Him. He said nothing to me. However, His Spirit let me know of His love for me. When I awakened, His love remained with me, and I have felt His love all of my life, especially at times of my deep pain and sorrow.

When my sister tormented me, I continued to love her. One time, after she hurt me, I took all the coins I had from my piggy bank. There were pennies, nickels, dimes, and a few quarters. I gathered the coins, counted them, walked to town (one mile from our home), and went to the five-and-ten-cent store and searched for a gift that I had enough money to purchase. I went home and gave the gift to my sister. She didn't say "thank you." I wasn't offended. I was just happy that I did something kind for her.

When thunderstorms appeared (and that was often in Oklahoma), the sky would become so dark with clouds, and from one end of the sky to the other, there were streaks of lightning with very loud thunder. When I heard the thunder, I had the feeling that Jesus was talking to me to let me know He was there. I really enjoyed that feeling.

When I was very young, I looked up at the sky. I knew I had been with my Savior before I came to this earth, and I was to live my life so I could one day go back to live with my Father in heaven. (Nobody had taught me these things. I just knew it.) When I was investigating the Church of Jesus Christ of Latter-Day Saints, the first thing I was taught was about the "preexistence." That everyone was living in the preexistence as a spirit. We came to earth to get a body to house our spirit and live worthy to gain eternal life.

There was a piece of property that was a block and a half away from our home. I often walked there. Nobody lived on that property. There was a stream of water that ran through that land. Also, I loved seeing the trees and wildflowers. I found peace within my soul, and I prayed to my Savior and thank Him for the creation.

There were many plum trees in our backyard. I would go and lay down between the plum trees with my ukulele, look up at the fleecy white clouds in the sky, see pictures with my imagination within the clouds, sing, and play my ukulele. I would often talk to my Savior and express my gratitude to Him for being there with me and for me.

(Later in this book, you will learn about Roy.)

After Roy (my husband) and I were married, I became a convert to the Church of Jesus Christ of Latter-Day Saints. Kennecott Copper was where Roy worked. Kennecott went on strike. The strike lasted nine months. Roy began working right away in Hawthorne, Nevada. Because of my illness, he returned to Ely where I was hospitalized. We lived in McGill, Nevada. He got a job with a rancher. Then he filled out some resumes and submitted them to a few places for a steady job. After Kennecott's strike was over, Roy received an offer to work with the state of Nevada, Fish and Game.

Roy walked into our home in McGill, Nevada, and I was sitting down with our son that was close to one year of age. He asked me, "How would you like to move to Sunnyside, Nevada?"

I thought he was joking with me. I answered, "Sure, why not?"

He was serious. I had a business in Ely, Nevada. It was a place where people could come for exercise to lose weight and become healthier—Rozena's Slenderella Salon. I sold the business and began to pack our bags for the move to Sunnyside.

We lived in a home which was owned by the state of Nevada. His job began in March of 1969. Our son, Randal, was born April 4, 1968, which made him very close to one year of age.

Roy's paycheck was not much to live on. I was the one that took care of our finances. Randal came down with pneumonia. It was during the weekend. We drove him sixty-seven miles to Ely, Nevada. That required taking him to the hospital emergency room. Another time, his temperature was 105 degrees. Again, it was on a weekend. So once more, we took him to the hospital in Ely. It took a great deal of budgeting our money to get through these experiences.

Fifteen months after giving birth to Randal, we had another son. He lived twelve and a half hours and died. There were funeral expenses. Another fifteen months, we had our third son, Ray.

Our insurance was not the best. We had medical bills to doctors, hospitals, and prescriptions, as well as the funeral home to pay. Of course, we needed food, gas for traveling to any place we had to go such as church meetings, shopping for food, etc. Every place we went, it was a very long, round trip. Roy received a calling from the church to be a home teacher for a family that lived at Blue Eagle. That was very far to travel from Sunnyside, especially round trip. Roy was told that it was sufficient to just mail a card to the family to let them know he cared for them. However, when the husband/father came down with a back problem, he couldn't put up his hay. Roy, being the sweetheart that he is, traveled back and forth from our home to their home until the hay was taken care of. I was not happy with Roy because of the gas that was necessary to drive that far multiple times.

*****

Roy and I had our marriage sealed in the St. George Temple a little over one year following our civil marriage. We were so happy, and it was such a blessing that our children were born under covenant.

I had a strong testimony of the Church of Jesus Christ of Latter-Day Saints. I had searched for a very long time and gone to different denominations to find the church I could truly believe their teachings. I felt so blessed that we had gone to the temple to have our marriage sealed for time and all eternity. However, I began to have negative thoughts about the temple. I talked with Roy about my feelings. He advised me to go and talk with our bishop. I did just that. The bishop bore a beautiful testimony about the gospel of Jesus Christ. I left his office thinking that was such a good meeting, but that was his testimony…not mine.

As I returned home, I knew I had one thing I could do. I had such a deep devotion and love for my Savior, Jesus Christ. I would go to Him for my answer. I began to fast. I had no food or water for twenty-four hours. I prayed constantly. I knew I had not received an answer. Without breaking my fast, I fasted another day. I experienced the same problem at the end of the second day. So I fasted the third day. At the end of the third day, I felt as though the heaven had opened up for me. Thoughts filled my heart and soul to let me know I had gone through the negative experience because I had failed to pay a full and honest tithing. Also, that I had failed to support my husband with his church calling. I was told to put my faith and trust in Jesus Christ, follow His teachings, and witness the blessings that would come to me, my husband, and our children, and we would receive our needs. Needless to say, the next paycheck that arrived, I paid the 10 percent tithing that the gospel teaches to do. I was amazed and appreciative at how I was able to pay bills, shop for food, etc. I have paid tithing ever since.

Years later, I went through another test about paying tithing. After retiring, Roy and I moved to Lund, Nevada. We were not on Medicare yet. I fell and broke my hip. I was flown to Las Vegas, received a surgery, etc. The same year, Roy was flown to Salt Lake City because the doctor in Ely thought he had a serious heart problem. It turned out to be his gallbladder. We were very much in debt because of the cost for the two emergency flights. I drew out our savings to pay for the flights, ambulances, etc. That put us in a higher income bracket, so the IRS received the remainder that we had in our savings.

Again, I was faced with not having enough money to pay our monthly bills along with our tithing. I remembered the experience I had when we lived at Sunnyside and wrote out a check for tithing. Of course, I didn't have money to pay our monthly bills. A couple of days went by, and Roy received a phone call from a man that had a new ranch in Lund. He needed a man to manage his ranch. So many people told him that Roy would be a good man for the job. He told Roy that if he took the job, he would send him one thousand dollars in advance. Roy took the job. The check was received the next day. Our bills were paid on time, and we had money left over.

I have learned that when "fear" enters my mind, I must immediately get rid of the thought about fear, and instead of being afraid, put my faith and trust in Jesus Christ. That takes away my fear and gives peace to my soul.

Everyone can do the same to receive blessings from the Lord. The most important thing is that we live worthy of what the scriptures teach us. We know that we must do His will and not rationalize to do our will. I believe in Jesus Christ. Most importantly, *I believe Him.*

> Let the words of my mouth
> And the meditation of my heart
> Be acceptable in thy sight, oh Lord
> My strength and my Redeemer. (Psalm 19:14)

CHAPTER 7

MISTAKE OF MY LIFE THAT GREW INTO A PROFESSIONAL SINGING CAREER

During the summer between my junior and senior year of high school, I met a man that just returned home from his military service. He was seven years older than me, very good looking, and owned a Harley-Davidson motorcycle. He took me on several trips with his Harley. He asked me to marry him. I talked with my mother, and she told me, "If that's what you want, do it." She had no interest in planning a wedding. She didn't even go to the marriage.

So I got married.

There was no honeymoon. As a matter of fact, the marriage began with a broken heart. I found myself sitting at home alone each weekend. During the weeks, it was necessary that my husband went to work. Everything changed when he disappeared Friday nights. I experienced being alone until Sunday evenings. There was no explanation. It was as though I had no say in the matter. This was repeated every weekend.

I was washing clothes on the first Monday morning after our marriage. As I emptied the Levi's pockets that belonged to my husband to do the wash, I found condoms. When I asked about them, I was given black eyes and a busted lip.

I stayed in the marriage for one year and three months. There were more domestic violence experiences. I don't desire to go into the details. It would be as though I am going through the suffering again.

I filed for divorce. During the marriage, I finished high school via correspondence. I immediately signed up for attending a junior college at Wilburton, Oklahoma. At the time, the college was called Eastern Oklahoma A and M. The name has been changed to Eastern Oklahoma State College.

My classes were intermediate typing, intermediate shorthand, office machine training, speech, and English 101. I actually made the dean's honor roll.

My parents and I drove to Dallas, Texas, to visit with relatives.

I went to KRLD-TV, walked in, and talked with the receptionist, and after I told her I was there for an audition, she called John Hicks and gave him the message from his friend that he was to give me an audition. John Hicks was in the back of the station preparing for a live TV show to air. I was taken back to meet Hicks. Mother sat down at the piano and played the introduction to the song "A Tear Fell" by Theresa Brewer. After I sang, I was added as a guest to the show. After the show, I was taken to meet Howard McLemore, and he asked me to sign a five-year contract to sing professionally. Before I signed the contract, I explained I was enrolled in college, and I would need to finish the semester before I could begin my singing career. I was told, "Rozena, just sign the contract, finish the semester, and return to Dallas to begin your career."

I completed my semester of college and returned to Dallas. I got a job working for New York Life Insurance until my first assignment to sing came through. I told the manager at the Insurance Company that I would only be with them until I got the message from McLemore that it was time for me to begin singing. So I worked as a stenographer for four months. My first job as a singer was in Abilene, Texas, to costar with the Hilltoppers at the Sand's Hotel. My singing engagements were booked through Music Corporation of America.

I was so excited for my first engagement. I was treated like a star. There was a nice room where professionals applied my makeup and fixed my hair. I was given new clothes for my performance. Needless to say, I had butterflies before I performed. However, when the music began, and I opened my mouth to sing. Thank goodness I felt very relaxed.

My next job was in Dallas at the Cipango. It was a multimillionaire's private club. That job lasted nine months. I performed with the George Gadosh Combo. Gadosh was one of the best saxophonist I had ever heard. I learned, very quickly, that I was to sing seven nights a week. There were many celebrities I entertained during my stay there. A few of the names were John Wayne, Perry Como, Frankie Lane, etc. I am enclosing a few pictures of my stay during those nine months at the Cipango. It is no longer in existence. However, it can be brought up on the internet to read about when it was in operation. The Cipango was known as having the best food anywhere. Only trouble was, people could only go there if they were a member or knew a member and was invited. I was fortunate to eat my dinner there every evening. Just thinking about it brings back memories of how fantastic the food was.

My next experience was going on tours. I recall being told I would be touring with orchestras from the "big band days." These tours were the last of those performances. When MCA told me I would be going on a sixteen-state tour with Ted Weems, I was astonished. The first job with Ted Weems, we had just finished our first performance of the first set, and he came to me to hand me some maracas and told me to play them during the Spanish music. I told him I didn't know how to play the maracas. He said, "Do you want me to send you to get a degree to play the maracas?" He had me take them and said, "Play them."

During our break, a musician came to me and told me he heard the entire conversation between Ted Weems and me. The musician told me there were little beads inside the maracas. I was to hold the maracas and use my wrist to make the beads sound crisp as the maracas were being played. Then he showed me how to play for a samba. He said, "Shake the maracas up and down." And he showed me how to play them for the Spanish bolero and other different rhythms.

I told him, "You can't imagine how much I appreciate you showing me how to play the maracas." When the orchestra was back and the music began, it wasn't long before I was to play those maracas. I got up and had so much fun playing them I began to dance along while playing the maracas. Ted Weems was happy. For anyone that doesn't know about Ted Weems, he became famous in his day by having the song "Heartaches" reach the number one rating multiple times. Elmo Tanner was the whistler in the recording for "Heartaches" and during tours. Tanner also whistled for the popular song in those days called "Nola." I shall never forget the thrill I had to sing with this fantastic orchestra behind me. It gave me chills as I sang.

One thing I learned during that sixteen-state tour is I had to look on the stationery of each hotel room where I stayed to recall which town I was in because we traveled to a different place to perform each night. There was continuous traveling. Another thing I realized is there was a Bible in my room of each hotel. I would be so tired after each performance I would go to my room and read a scripture or two of the Bible to relax and sleep well before being on the road again.

I memorized the Psalm 23: "The Lord is my shepherd." This was such a blessing for me. I repeated it often within my own mind if I were frightened or happy. It just helped me to feel I was never alone. I always had "my Savior" to accompany me day and night. Then I read Matthew, Mark, Luke, and John over and over. I felt so much joy just to see birds fly, beautiful trees, or flowers and to pass by a person and smile and say "Hello." It also made me desire to find a gospel I could truly believe the teachings. I didn't have time to attend a church because of traveling constantly. However, that changed later on during my singing career. Very seldom was I privileged to go to any church because of traveling and entertaining on Sundays. When I did go to church, I didn't care what denomination it was because I was looking for the church I could believe to be true.

I toured with more big band leaders such as Charley Barnett, known for the song "Cherokee."

Glenn Miller died in 1944. Tex Beneke was asked by Miller's widow to take Glenn Miller's orchestra's book on the road again beginning the year 1946. Beneke was born the year 1914. He joined Glenn Miller's band in 1938. I toured with Tex Beneke's (Glenn Miller's book) around 1962. Some of the songs that were played during the tour were "Chattanooga Choo-Choo," "In the Mood,"

HE RESTORETH MY SOUL

"Midnight Serenade," etc. What a privilege it was for me to be the singer for Tex Beeker.

Claude Thornhill, orchestra leader, composed and played the jazz and pop standards "Snowfall" and "I Wish I Had You." I sang with Thornhill and his orchestra at the Peabody Hotel in Memphis, Tennessee, a couple of times. The Peabody is a great place to entertain. There is a beautiful room with a very large dance floor near the orchestra, and the dining area is elevated above the dance floor. I recall the beautiful dining room had lace tablecloths, candles, chandeliers, etc. After the dining, the large orchestra goes from the dining area to outside on the upper floor of the hotel, and the guests dance to the beautiful music of the orchestra under the starlit sky, with an atmosphere for a wonderful, relaxing evening.

Another interesting atmosphere at the Peabody are the ducks that stay in a pen on the roof and come down in the elevator during the morning hours, walk across the lobby floor, and get in the fountain to remain during the entire day, then walk back across the lobby floor to the elevator and return to the pen on the roof. My room at the Peabody had colonial style (like new) furniture. They also had a pitcher that was kept in a bowl like people used years ago. It was my favorite place during the entire seven years that I sang professionally.

I do want to tell you a very interesting thing that happened to me during the time I was in Memphis. It was on a Sunday morning. I had the day off. I got up early, got dressed, and drove to find a church to attend. I didn't care which denomination it was; I just wanted to go to church. I drove until I found a pretty little white church that was located on top of a hill. They had a good parking area. As I walked to the church from my car, I could hear music coming through the air from the church. I walked up the stairs into the church. Everyone turned and looked at me. The people were all black. I found myself a seat on the very back row.

As I sat there, the preacher got up and said the twenty-third Psalm, one line at a time, and had the congregation repeat after each line he spoke. This brought tears to my eyes (as I had memorized this very special scripture when I toured with Ted Weems' orchestra). A sermon followed. I shall never forget what the preacher said.

The words were, "Beware of wolves in sheep clothing. The devil can come up in disguise. He can drive up in a big, long Cadillac car. (As he spoke about the wolves in sheep clothing, he strutted across the stage.) As he discontinued his sermon, he got up and asked me to come up to say what I came to say. He thought I was a social worker.

I stood up from where I was sitting and used my loud voice so everyone could hear me and said, "I am in Memphis, singing at the Peabody Hotel. I had a Sunday off, so I decided to drive until I found a church to attend. As I came upon this beautiful church on a hill, I parked, and as I walked up to your church, I heard the most beautiful music you were singing. I walked into your church and found a place to sit on the back row. The twenty-third Psalm is my very favorite scripture, and it brought tears to my eyes to take part in repeating the words with all of you. I totally enjoyed the sermon, and it's a good thing for all of us to take the words to heart. I know there are two kinds of people in this world. People are either good, or they are bad. I have found nothing but 'good' here among each of you." I told them I would *forever* remember this special visit with them.

The preacher closed the meeting and asked me to stand with him at the door as everyone left. I stood with him. Everyone shook my hand as they went out the door.

Another special memory of Memphis is Elvis Presley's dad, Vernon, and second wife, Dee, came to the Peabody Hotel for dining and dancing while I was singing there. It was Saturday night. Sunday, after I had gone to the church I just mentioned, I drove to Graceland. It was my birthday. I was at the gate as Elvis drove by. He called the gate and invited me to come to the house. I couldn't believe what was happening. I was there the remainder of the day. It was so fun to tour his home. In some of the rooms, there were mirrors on the ceiling. He showed me his barber room in his home where his hair was groomed. I was very impressed with his white baby grand piano, which was close to the entrance of his home. He played the piano and sang.

He had a mynah bird that was in a large cage in the kitchen. Elvis offered me a peanut butter and banana sandwich as he prepared one for himself. I turned it down. If it had been peanut butter and jam, I certainly would have accepted. He treated me so special. He learned it was my birthday, and he actually rented an entire theatre where he took all of his friends to see a movie. I was privileged to sit right by Elvis during the movie. To this day, I cannot remember what movie was playing. The biggest thrill is the birthday kiss he gave me. As I left his home and drove back to the Peabody, I was feeling like it was all a dream. I'm so glad it wasn't a dream. Not long after my visit, Elvis and Priscilla were married. Of course, I never saw Elvis again. However, the one visit gave me a lifelong memory.

I had a booking at the Montague Hotel in Houston, Texas. I was invited to appear on a TV show to advertise my singing there. The TV show was over at noon. I was driving back to the hotel on the main highway. There was a woman driving a Buick that ran a Stop sign from the street that intercepted the highway where I was driving. She ran into my car. I was injured and taken to the hospital. After much testing, there were a few physicians that gathered around my hospital bed. I was told, "Rozena, you will not be singing anymore. You will have to find another profession. You have a severe jaw injury and will be lucky if you will be able to talk plainly again." I absolutely could not believe what I was hearing.

I was once again, in Oklahoma, in my parents' home. My mouth was wired shut. I began to regurgitate. I could not get the wires clipped and thought I was going to choke to death. Daddy finally got the wires cut. A physician drained fluid from my jaw and it automatically locked my jaw closed. I was finally able to begin physical therapy. I began saying my alphabet. I had to repeat "A" over and over. Then I went to "B" and continued throughout the alphabet. It took forever. It was difficult to keep my faith alive. I'm not sure how long it took me to go through the entire alphabet. However, I had trouble saying the *S* letter. I got to where I could say it. It just wasn't very plain.

I called my agent from Music Corporation of America and told him I was ready to sing again. I was booked at the King's Club in the Adolphus Hotel. Don Neely was the piano player and leader of the combo. I told him what I had been going through, and he knew I was still having trouble with the letter *S*. So how did he handle that problem? He gave me an arpeggio to "Side by Side." Not only once a night, but each time the crowd changed to a different group of people. I was so unhappy to be forced to sing a song with so many *Ss*. That was the best thing he could have done for me. It didn't take long for me to not even think about having to sing an "S."

I was happy to have proven those doctors in Houston wrong. I was singing once more!

A place I truly enjoyed was in Scottsdale, Arizona. I was booked at The Executive Inn. There was a piano player named Bob Voss. Bob and I were the only two entertaining at the Executive Inn. He was, by far, the best pianist I had ever worked with. With his accompaniment, I could sing my songs and feel them coming from my entire heart and soul. There was a crowd of people there every night. What a wonderful booking. Bob wanted me to remain with him to entertain as a "pair." I wanted, too, so badly. However, I didn't because of the crowd of people he associated with. It literally frightened me so badly I could not feel comfortable being around Bob and his friends. I will always remember him and believe the two of us could have made it to the top of the entertainment chart. I was given extra special reviews as we entertained, and we were asked to stay there to entertain indefinitely. I just couldn't do it.

I was booked with Joe Barber and his combo at Baton Rouge, Louisiana, at the Spinosa's Supper Club. That was a fun location. For one thing, I recall the freshly grown and then roasted peanuts. People were so nice, and the peanuts were warm and so delicious. I learned I couldn't say anything about my favorite things, such as talking about how I enjoyed fried green tomatoes. I was with a crowd of people there, and the next day, the bellboy was knocking at my door with a large tray of delicious fried green tomatoes. I was invited to follow Arnold Palmer around the golf course during a tournament. That was surely a treat.

Another place I was booked with Joe Barber and his combo was Corpus Christi, Texas. There were cottages on the beach where each musician in the combo had their own cottage, and I had mine. We entertained at what was called "The Water Club," which was located on Water Street. Such a nice place to work. And the beach!

Wow! There was a big boat called "The Sally Dee." On my day off, I took The Sally Dee to the Gulf of Mexico, and so far, you could not see land. They had a "kitty" where you could put money, and if you caught the biggest "eatable" fish, you would win the "kitty." I thought I had it won with the sea bass that I caught until someone caught a bigger fish than I had at the end of the day. It required having a rod and reel that could handle reeling in a very large fish right up to the boat, and guys were there with big fish nets that would bring the fish onto the boat. There were a lot of stingrays caught and also hammerhead sharks. Wow!

Even on the days we worked at the club, we would go out on the jetty to catch small fish that we cut up and used as bait to put on a line to throw out into the Gulf of Mexico and catch big crabs. We threw the rope out as far as we could and left it in one place in the water until you could feel a tug from a crab getting on the bait. Then you pulled the rope a small distance until you felt the crab tug again. That continued until the crab was right up to the jetty. This was after we were off work, so it was very dark. It required us to have a bright light and use a net to get the crab and put it in a bucket. One thing I learned is if you have only one crab in your bucket, you stand a chance of losing your crab, which would crawl out of the bucket. However, if you have two crabs in the bucket and one tries to get out, the crab on the bottom will pull the one on top back into the bucket. I kept a big pan of water on my stove to drop the crab in boiling water until it was done. I had nutcrackers to get the meat from the crab's legs, dip it in melted butter, and enjoy the delicious meal.

What a fun place it was to be in Corpus Christi. Another day off, the wives of the combo and I drove to Padre Island. There was a ferry we drove my car on, and it took us to the island. We had our swim suits on. There was nobody else around the area where we were. I had my strong rod and reel I had purchased and began walking out into the Gulf of Mexico. I wasn't in the water very long when a great big fish, not far from where I was standing, jumped out of the water. I got out of that water as quickly as I possibly could. If that fish had gotten on my line, I thought I would have been a goner. I was back on the beach in no time.

There were many bubbles coming out of the sand. I took both my hands and scooped up the sand to see what was causing the bubbles. I brought up handfuls of tiny shells with pastel shades of different colors. I put them in a box and took them back to Corpus Christi. I packaged them up and sent them to my parents in Oklahoma. They got a beautiful and very large seashell in which they filled with the small shells to display them for their friends to see. There were many other places where I was booked to entertain. I have selected the places I enjoyed the most.

Now, there is another side of my singing. My agent called me in to ask me if I would consider singing Western music. Billy Grey worked with Hank Thompson for years and then hired a band of his own. Panther Hall was opening for the first time. Panther Hall was located in Fort Worth, Texas. Billy Grey needed a singer. So I agreed to go to Fort Worth and sing for the opening. Billy Grey asked me to stay with his band and travel with them. They had a regular gig with the Golden Nugget in Las Vegas and traveled to many places. I accepted the invitation.

One interesting place where we were booked was the US Air Force base which was located in Labrador at Goose Bay. We flew to Montreal, Canada, where we changed planes to head for Labrador. That was certainly an interesting trip. To begin with, at Montreal airport, my luggage was checked by opening it, having hands reaching into my suitcase, and quickly flinging my clothes out of the bag, and when they were satisfied nothing was inside that shouldn't be there, they proceeded to pick up my clothes and throw them back inside my suitcase. I was so particular about my packing. I even ironed my underthings. My clothes were cleaned, ironed, and packed so they would be ready to be on the stage to entertain when we arrived at Goose Bay. My face must have been so red from being upset. Somehow, I lived through that ordeal.

In Labrador, there are interesting memories. There are only a few months in the year that snow isn't on the ground. We were there a few weeks. I saw very tall markers on each side of the roads. I asked what they were for. I was told the markers had been installed so people would not lose their way when they traveled with the dogs pulling the sleds during the winter.

Ollie and Orv invited the whole band to their house for dinner on our day off. They had a big pen where they kept a lot of dogs that pulled the sled through the snow. I went up to the fence so I could have a closer look at the dogs. Orv quickly yelled, "Get away from the dogs! They don't like to be close to a person that is small in size." I was five feet four inches and weighed 110 pounds, so I was a no-no. I didn't have to be asked twice. Right away, I went back into the house.

I got acquainted with a mounted policeman. He took me places in Labrador I wouldn't have been able to see if he hadn't taken me. There was a beautiful area that looked like where the Clydesdale horse's commercial advertising Budweiser beer was filmed. The blue water, the snow-capped mountains, the spruce trees—oh, how beautiful. I didn't need to take a picture…that scene will stay within my soul forever.

The day we flew out of Labrador, the snow was coming down so fast. We could barely see to board the plane. I was praying we wouldn't be snowed in for the year. The pilot knew what he was doing, and all was well.

Billy Grey had a regular TV show in Dallas, Texas—The Louisiana Hayride. I was a regular on that show. One day, Bob Wills was a guest on the show. He asked me if I would go to Carson City, Nevada, to be a guest on his show for a couple of weeks. He asked me if I could yodel. He said that was a requirement for me to be his singer. I told him, "Yes, I can yodel."

He asked me to sing "Bet You My Heart, I Love You." That was a fun song to sing. I was one of the last singers to appear with Bob Wills.

I was under contract to record records for Longhorn Records. Dewey Groom and his wife, Gwen, were the owners of The Longhorn Ballroom in Dallas. The ballroom was as large as a city block. He had a large Western band. Many famous celebrities entertained there, such as Willie Nelson, Roy Clark, and many, many, others. I sang with Dewey's band in between traveling to promote my recordings.

Gwen made me several glittery Western outfits that I wore with my pearl-coated Western boots. She was a very special lady.

Dewey Groom said, "Rozena, you are going to Ely, Nevada, to sing with Speedy Ross's band to promote your newly released record."

I asked Dewey Groom, "Where in the world is Ely, Nevada?" I thought that Ely had to be one of the smallest towns that nobody had ever heard of. The Nevada Hotel is where I would be singing. It was the Fourth of July, and I was to be there for one week. A friend of mine, LaVerne Peoples, took a vacation, so she could make the trip with me. We booked our flight from Dallas, Texas, to Las Vegas, Nevada. Who would ever have thought we would have trouble getting from Las Vegas to Ely?

I only had so much time to reach Ely for my first appearance. I learned there was no bus, no train, and no flight, and Ely had no car rental. I could have flown to Salt Lake City and from there, take a small aircraft to Ely, or I could have flown to Reno and take a small aircraft to Ely. Only problem is… I would have gone past my deadline to reach Ely if I had taken the route to either Salt Lake City or Reno. I knew a friend that was entertaining in Las Vegas. He couldn't drive me to Ely because he was working that night. He had a friend that was also working in Vegas but was on a day off. My friend allowed his friend to drive his car and take LaVerne and me to Ely. Bless his heart, he saved the day. I made it to the stage and on time. Whew! Speedy Ross had a great combo, and I enjoyed working with them.

I am going to back track a little. I was traveling through Salt Lake City about three years prior to singing in Ely. As I drove through Salt Lake City, I passed by the LDS Temple. I didn't know what the building was. However, the feelings within my heart caused me to wonder why I felt so drawn to the building. I asked about the building and was told it was the temple of the Church of Jesus Christ of Latter-Day Saints. I never forgot the feeling that came over me as though I had a magnet inside me that drew me to that temple. The reason I am mentioning this experience is as follows: When I first started singing professionally, and I was traveling, I decided when I met a good-looking young man that showed an interest in me and had a great personality, I told myself that man could be a serial killer for all I knew, and it was in my best interest to not allow myself to get close to any man that might hurt me in any way.

Well, a young man walked into the Nevada Hotel casino where I was entertaining. I looked at him and immediately had the same feeling I had when I passed by the LDS Temple in Salt Lake City. My spirit felt there was a magnet drawing me to this stranger. For a few minutes, I stood still on that stage just looking at him. It was as though I forgot I was even on the stage to entertain. On my break, LaVerne and I went to the coffee shop of the Nevada Hotel. This young man and the bartender came in to the coffee shop together and sat down across the aisle and a few booths down from where we were sitting. I told LaVerne what had happened to me when he walked into the room when I was performing. LaVerne said to me, "I wondered what happened to you. I saw you just standing there on stage, and that certainly wasn't like you. Well, there he is. Why don't you go over and ask him what his name is?"

I said, "I couldn't do that!"

Her answer was, "If you don't, I'm going to go ask him for you." I knew LaVerne would do just as she said. I sure didn't want that to happen, so I walked over to his booth.

I ask Joe, the bartender, "Joe, why don't you introduce me to your friend?"

Joe replied, "Sure, what's your name?"

(The bar where Joe worked was right next to the stage where I was performing. My name was on the neon-lit sign outside on the entrance of the Nevada Hotel, and a very large picture of me with my name on it was at the entrance of the room, where I was entertaining. And Joe was working each night I had been entertaining where my name was mentioned over and over. I felt so embarrassed that he didn't know my name. The only thing I could do was tell Joe my name.)

So Joe introduced me to Roy Horsley. When Joe had to go back to the bar to work, I went back into the casino to sing. Roy followed. Roy sat in a booth close to where I was singing. When my set was through, I went over, and Roy and I became acquainted. I learned he was going through a rough time because his friend had just been killed in an airplane crash. I felt so badly for the sadness he was feeling. Because of his mourning, the conversation turned to religion. Roy told me he was a member of the Church of Jesus Christ of Latter-Day Saints. He said he wasn't active in the church and hadn't been for quite a while, but he had been baptized when he was eight years of age.

I asked him, "What were the teachings of the church?"

He said that they believed in "the word of wisdom." He explained that drinking alcohol or smoking was not good for a body. Roy was sitting there drinking a beer. I was drinking orange juice (which was always my drink when I was entertaining).

Roy asked me if he could come to the hotel the next day, and he would show me around Ely. I agreed. I was wearing a black casual dress, high-heeled shoes, my hair was styled into an updo, my makeup was on, and I was ready for our date. He drove me to the corral that was one of his favorite places to go in Ely. There were horses and Roy's cowboy friends. I was certainly not dressed for being at the corral. However, I didn't act like it was inconvenient. Roy began roping a bucket. His cowboy friends suggested that Roy teach me to rope the bucket. Roy gave me instructions, I tried, and guess what? I roped the bucket. When he drove me back to the hotel, he stopped to let me out. Because of the traffic and there was no parking spot, I told him I would just get out from my side of his car. He reached over and gave me a quick kiss, and I went into the hotel with deep feelings for Roy.

I just knew Roy would come back to the hotel the following night. However, that didn't happen. I was crushed. The next day, I walked down the street of Ely, looking into the windows of the businesses. I was window-shopping, and I don't recall a thing I was looking at. All my mind could think about was Roy. I went into a pharmacy across the street from the Nevada Hotel. I found a card that had a picture of the back of a little girl and a little boy sitting on a fence together. The words were: "I'll Luv You," then you open the card, which said "Till the Cows Come Home." I then found a little stuffed yellow cow that was wearing a red flower on its head. I put the card and cow in a bag with my Dallas, Texas, address and my phone number. I took it to Joe and asked him to please give it to Roy when he sees him. He must have seen him quickly because Roy showed up that night. I got to talk with him before I left Ely to head back to Las Vegas so we could board our flight to Dallas. I left Ely, but I didn't leave without Roy on my mind "constantly."

Roy called me often. That was the day when payphones were popular. One time, he had gotten a roll of quarters and called me from the Nevada Hotel. As we talked, I could hear the quarters go all over the floor. That had to be a job to pick them up. He told me he was planning a trip to Dallas, Texas, to see me. I was so thrilled. As a matter of fact, I would sing on stage, and on my break, I would go to my dressing room, cry, fix my makeup, and go back to entertain again. I had told Roy I wouldn't date anyone. I would wait until we could be together again. Well, so much time went by I began to think we never would be together again. I told myself I should forget Roy because we would probably never see each other again. That night, Roy surprised me. He walked into the Longhorn Ballroom.

I took some time off, and Roy and I went to Oklahoma so he could meet my parents. We had to get back to Dallas because I didn't have very long to take a break with my job. Roy and I went to the Longhorn, and he sat and listened to me sing. Then we danced and talked about the love we both felt for each other. We talked of marriage. I mentioned to him if we were truly meant to be together, we should take a year to see how everything turns out. I was scheduled for a tour outside the USA. Roy left with feelings of love for me, and we agreed to not date anyone else. We would be always thinking of each other. It was all I could do to sing after he left.

I thought Roy was on his way back to Nevada. Before the night was over, he had turned around and came back to the Longhorn Ballroom. He asked me to dance with him. As we danced, we both felt the deep love for each other. I looked into his eyes, and I felt his spirit looking into mine. We decided that we wouldn't wait. That we would set a date for our marriage. Dewey Groom wanted us to come to his office. He said, "Rozena, everyone gets married. You don't walk away from your career. I have heard that is what you are planning to do."

I told Dewey, "I know our marriage would never stay together if I am traveling constantly. I will walk away from my career."

After I went back on stage, Dewey talked to Roy and tried to convince him to think it over and see I must continue to sing professionally. Dewey could have sued me because I had signed a contract to record three records a year for a three-year period. Dewey did give us his blessing and didn't sue me. I was given a shower at the Longhorn, and everyone gave me their blessing. I took time to make my wedding dress. The material was a white soft full-length dress. LaVerne made my veil. My cousin, Tommy, from Kentucky drove to Oklahoma to get my parents, and the three of them came to Dallas. Mother rode to Nevada with me, and Daddy rode to Nevada with Tommy. We were married at the Church of Jesus Christ of Latter-Day Saints in October 2, 1965. It was a lovely small wedding.

HE RESTORETH MY SOUL

Rozena Eads

The Chordettes

Rozena performing at Scottsdale, Arizona Executive Inn

HE RESTORETH MY SOUL

HITS   "Only You"   "Heartaches"

"Three Coins in the Fountain" sung by The Four Aces

Rozena with Billy Grey and the Golden Nuggets

ROZENA CAROLINE HORSLEY

Rozena Eads, Hartshorne singer, poses prettily in her costume while appearing in the Longhorn Ranch Ballroom at Dallas. In addition to appearing regularly in the Dallas club, Rozena has been making records and recently returned to Dallas after a two-week engagement in Carson City, Nevada with Bob Wills and his Western band.

Roy and Rozena's Wedding

CHAPTER 8

ROY

I met Roy during the July fourth celebration in Ely, Nevada. The year was 1965. I have mentioned Roy in my book several times. Roy is the person on this earth who has given me my life's happiness.

When I saw Roy for the very first time, he was very handsome, and to look into his eyes, I knew he was a good man. Roy and I have been married fifty-six years. We have three sons: Randal Lynn Horsley, married to Susan Jene' (Brandt) Horsley; Kevin Paul Horsley (deceased); and Ray Allen Horsley, married to RuthAnn (Simmons) Horsley.

We have two grandchildren. One is Brittanie Nicole (Horsley) Reid, who is married to Robert William Reid. They have three children: Berkley Ann Reid (age eight), Baylor Max Reid (age seven), and Bostyn Lux Reid (age three). Our grandson, Cyler Ray Horsley, is married to Evelyn Eve (Pitt) Horsley. They have one son named Killian Ray Horsley (age six.) This is a small number in people. However, this is a quality family. We are so blessed as a family and are sealed for time and eternity.

Roy has had so many accomplishments. He was a leader in FFA when he was in high school. He worked on different ranches. He worked for Kennecott Copper in McGill, Nevada, and during that time, he was a blacksmith apprentice. He was an employee of Nevada Department of Wildlife. He has a "retirement plaque" from the Department of Wildlife, which reads: "In Recognition of 30 years of outstanding service with Nevada Division of Wildlife, March 25, 1969 to July 11, 1999. From your co-workers."

Roy worked on the Wayne E Kirch Wildlife Management Area for four years, managed the Key Pittman Management Area for one year, managed the Overton Wildlife Management Area, and became the supervisor over the managers for Kirch, Key Pittman, and Overton.

After Roy's retirement, he received a letter from Fred Wright (Chief of Administration Services in 1979). Roy Horsley, Wildlife Area supervisor, appears in the list which can be viewed on the internet under Fred Wright Collection on the Nevada Department of Wildlife History. Roy was recognized for designing and implementing the OWMA Assigned Blind Reservation System. This reduced the impact on the OWMA resources. For years, there were too many hunters for the size of the area, and hunter success was very low. The reservation and assigned blind system increased hunter success. The comment from Fred Wright to Roy: "I want you to realize that your input will be recognized in the report, which will be housed at UNR Special Collections."

Roy assisted on many bighorn sheep capture projects, and elk and antelope trapping in Utah and Wyoming. He assisted on annual big game helicopter surveys when needed because he liked to fly.

Roy met Dan Hosford, a professional retriever trainer, while Roy and friend Bart Tanner traveled to Canada to hunt geese. Dan lived in Hayden Lake, Idaho, at the time and was hired to furnish retrievers at the Wild Goose Hunting Lodge for the owners' clients. Roy and Dan became good friends. Dan was looking for a place he could go to train during the winter. Roy invited him to come to the OWMA, which he did. Roy became interested in learning to train retrievers. He learned many things from Dan, and through the years, he added his own technic to the training. Dan gave Roy a black Labrador puppy. Roy named the dog Ruger and began training Ruger with Dan's help. Roy and Ruger entered many North American Hunter Retriever Association and AKC Hunt Tests. Ruger's registered name is "Mercy's Rascal Ruger." Mercy was Dan's personal dog and a fantastic retriever, the mother of Ruger, a Grand Master Retriever in NAHRA and AKC, and a member of the 1000 Point Club.

Roy was a member of the NAHRA, (North America Hunting Retriever Association) and was also the Southwest regional director. Ruger was an exceptional dog and loved the hunt tests. He became a Grand Champion Master Hunter Retriever in NAHRA and earned over 1,000 senior points, which qualified him to be a member of the 1000 Point Club in November 2002. Very few retrievers earn that privilege. Roy and Ruger were invited to participate in two Richard A. Wolters NAHRA Invitational (1999 and 2000) and also one in Rapidan, Virginia (1999), and one in Edmonton, Alberta, Canada (2000). Ruger qualified in all. Ruger also earned his master hunter title in AKC (American Kennel Club). Cambridge Who's Who recognizes Roy G. Horsley and Rock Canyon Kennels as honored members. Roy qualified for inclusion in the Cambridge Who's Who, Registry of Executives, Professionals and Entrepreneurs 2009–2010 Edition.

Signed by Mitchel S. Robbins/Chairman/CEO, Cambridge Who's Who.

Dan encouraged Roy to organize a NAHRA club, along with Dan's help and several others that trained with Roy and Dan. The Las Vegas Hunting Retriever Club was organized, and Roy was president for many years. It became a very successful club and is still active today.

Roy trained retrievers for many clients and trained several of his clients to handle their dogs at hunt tests. Roy loved to train the dogs and see them progress; it was training the owners to handle their dogs that was the challenge.

Ruger died when he was fourteen years old. Roy's memories of the days he was involved with training and hunting with Ruger will always be special. Roy and Ruger were certainly a superior team.

Roy also organized the Moapa Valley Chapter of Ducks Unlimited and served as president for many years. He worked hard, and because of his interest, many people pitched in to help have successful DU dinners and activities. There were many businesses as well as many people that donated items for the raffles, etc. Moapa Valley and the Las Vegas area supported Ducks Unlimited.

After moving to Lund, Roy purchased a registered quarter horse from Bar D quarter horses in Utah. He loved to help ranchers at branding time and move their cows over the mountain from Lund to their BLM allotments in Cave Valley. Roy loves to take trail rides with our granddaughter, Brittanie, and her horse Bannock.

Roy likes to work with wood. He made a beautiful dining room table from two-inch oak. There were bird feeders, a rocking horse, bookcases, plus many more items that he made. Roy was a great dad for Randal and Ray. He taught them to work hard, climb mountains, swim, hunt, ride horses, participate in 4-H. He supported them by going and watching them play T-Ball, baseball, basketball, football, and Randal in wrestling. They also took karate lessons. Roy attended their piano recitals when they played in the high school band and played their trumpets in jazz band.

Roy is currently president of the Lund Rodeo Association. He works hard to be sure it is a great success. This takes much of his time to be sure everything is taken care of in the very best way. There has been much improvement in the quality of the rodeo grounds and arena. He makes certain the money is accounted for and knows exactly where the funds have come from. It's no wonder he is successful. One of the best qualities he has is the fact he is not egotistical. He is humble and treats everyone as his friend. Everyone likes Roy.

Roy has been my friend throughout our marriage. We have worked together, played together, gone through hard times together, supported each other, gone to church together, prayed together, and have spent fifty-six years of marriage together. Our love has grown deeper and more wonderful each year. We are true companions.

Roy has served in many callings in the Church of Jesus Christ of Latter-Day Saints. Some have included: scoutmaster, counselor in two bishoprics, bishop, Young Men's president, stake high council, ward mission leader, stake mission president for the Logandale Nevada Stake, Sunday school teacher, etc.

Roy absolutely loves our grandchildren, Brittanie and Cyler, their spouses, Robby Reid and Eve Horsley. He is great with our great-grandchildren, Berkley, Baylor, Bostyn, and Killian. They all love their "papa."

When I have been ill, Roy pitches in and helps me. He takes such good care of me. He cooks, cleans, makes sure I take my medicine, and certainly treats me with love. No words will ever be able to express my appreciation and love for this man.

Words cannot explain the depth of love I have for Roy. We are married for time and all eternity. I look forward to being with Roy forever.

Roy G. Horsley

Roy G. Horsley
Retriever Trainer

Ruger
Grand Champion Hunter Retriever
NAHRA

Roy and Rozena Horsley

CHAPTER 9

Honeymoon in the Mountains

Nobody told me how important hunting season is in Lund, Nevada. I found out in a hurry. Roy was born into a family that wouldn't miss deer hunting for anything! Of course, the hunt would begin in October. So the honeymoon was in the mountains. Roy and I slept in front part of a two-horse trailer. You can imagine how small that was.

Roy and I were on horseback going down a trail. He told me, "Honey, I want you to ride straight down the trail until you come to a place called Pothole Springs. I am going to ride over an area of the mountain to see if I can find a deer. I will meet you at the Pothole Springs." I thought that sounded easy enough. Problem is, I knew nothing about horses. It didn't take long before the cinch became loose. After I had ridden down the trail for a while, the saddle had tilted to the right, and I was not sitting straight up. I thought, *I watched Roy saddle the horse early this morning. I believe I can remember how he tightened the cinch.* Therefore, I got off the horse, tightened the cinch, and I forgot that Roy had helped me get into the saddle when we began our ride. I was too short to stretch my foot to the height of the stirrup. I tried a few times and learned it was no use.

It was obvious the horse could sense that I was totally not used to riding horses. She began to move which made matters worse. I tried a few times and had a thought. I could turn the horse the opposite direction so I could stand higher up on the mountain while

Missy, the horse, would be standing lower on the path. I thought that would make it easier to get my foot in the stirrup. I tried a few times and failed. I decided the best thing for me to do was just walk and lead the horse to where we needed to go. I walked and walked and walked and walked. (Get the picture?) I began to get very upset. I was so tired. I wanted to try once more to get on the horse. That was a joke. So I walked the rest of the way to Pothole Springs.

After I arrived at the Pothole Springs, it wasn't long before Roy came riding up. To say the least, I was not good company.

That wasn't the end of the story. Hunting went on and on until Roy got his deer, which could only happen if saw a deer. He had me ride a horse with others who were riding while Roy was going a different direction. I thought he wanted to have a better chance at finding a deer. These men (as well as Roy) were real, honest-to-goodness cowboys I was riding with. I'll never forget coming to a place on the mountain where there was a wash between the mountains. It wasn't a big wash at all. However, it was necessary to have the horse jump across the wash. It reminded me of these crazy leaning tree cards that have ridiculous pictures of cowboys riding on a mountain and jumping across to another mountain. I was never so frightened in all my life for that experience.

Another time, Roy's parents drove to our home very early one morning. We were going hunting and camping with them that day. I came out of the house with a very warm (light blue) parka that I had purchased in Labrador. I had western pants that were also light blue. I had gotten up early to get my makeup on and combed my hair as I was use to styling it. When I came out of the house and went to their truck, Roy's dad made the comment that the horses were making sounds of whinnying because of me. Of course, everybody had to laugh.

Family members, were totally relaxed and enjoying every minute of camping. Roy and I were higher up on the mountain and headed for the camping area. The mountain was so steep with a lot of shale where we had to get off our horses and lead them down the mountain. It didn't help me at all to have acrophobia. My feet were sliding on the shale, and the horses were also sliding on the shale.

Thoughts came to my mind about the possibility of a horse falling. I was as frightened as I could be, and I tried to not complain or show how scared I was.

One thing for sure… I was happy to be married to Roy.

CHAPTER 10

THE MOST WELCOMED VISITOR

Roy and I were in our home in Ely. The doorbell rang. Roy answered the door. There was a man that introduced himself to Roy. He said, "My name is Blaine Jones. Are you Roy Horsley?"

Roy answered, "Yes, may I help you?"

Jones answered, "There is an investigators class beginning Sunday at the Church of Jesus Christ of Latter-Day Saints stake house. I came here to invite you and your new wife to join us."

Roy said, "Thank you. I will talk to my wife about it and decide if we will attend."

I told Roy, "I am going to the investigators class. I have been looking for a church I could learn about their beliefs for a long time. I have gone to different denominations, and so far, I haven't found a church that could satisfy the way I feel."

Roy said to me, "Well, I will go with you."

One year prior to that time, I was singing in Elko, Nevada, at the Commercial Hotel where there was a ten-foot-four white polar bear taxidermy named White King that stood inside the front door of the lobby. A man by the name of Oren Probert, who was the manager of the hotel at the time, gave me some pamphlets about the Church of Jesus Christ of Latter-Day Saints. After I read each pamphlet from cover to cover and had questions that needed answers, I went to talk to Oren Probert and learned he was out of town on a business trip, and that he wouldn't return until after I was back on the road to my next appearance. Therefore, with my schedule, I knew I would not have a chance to receive answers to my inquiring questions.

At the investigators class, I kept the questions coming. Every moment was precious. The very first question was answered by teaching about the preexistence. It was explained that we were all spirits of our Father in heaven in the preexistence. We lived there until we were sent to this earth to obtain a body that housed our spirit. This was very interesting to me because when I was a very small child, I use to look up at the sky, and I knew I had been there someplace, and I knew I was to live righteously on this earth to return back to where I had come from. *Nobody had ever taught me this. However, I knew this truth.* This immediately got my undivided attention.

Each time I ask another question, another answer was given. I was told which scripture to read and to pray about it. I read the scriptures, and I not only prayed; I fasted and prayed. I truly wanted to know the truth that my Savior would have me know. After all, He had been my very best friend throughout my life, and I loved Him. I wanted to check out this religion to see if it was the church that Christ Himself had established while He was on this earth.

I knew Roy had been a member of the church since he was eight years of age. Yes, it's true he wasn't active in the church and hadn't been for quite a while. However, I asked him questions after we left the investigators meetings each Sunday. Roy was working at Kennecott Copper at the time and had a lunch bucket with a high dome lid, so there was plenty of room for his lunch. What I didn't know was he put his small book of scriptures that had been given to him when he served in the national guard. I didn't realize this for some time when he was bearing his testimony in a church service.

During his testimony, he said that he found a place at work where he could be alone and read the scriptures, so he could answer my questions that I repeatedly ask when we were first married. He said he was having trouble understanding the scriptures, so he went into the boiler room at work during his lunch break. He knew nobody would come into the room while he was there. It was pitch dark in the room after he closed the door. He knelt down in prayer to let heavenly Father know he was having trouble understanding the scriptures, and he needed help. At first, he was frightened because of a negative spirit being there. Then, a strong spirit was with him, and he felt at ease. He began to understand the scriptures, and during the weeks we were going to the investigator meetings, he was truly converted to the gospel.

As mentioned in this book, we were married October 2, 1965. I was converted to the gospel during the investigators classes as Roy became active, advanced in the priesthood, and baptized me January 1, 1966 (New Year's Day). We had our marriage sealed in the St. George Temple one year and three months later. Our first child was born April 4, 1968; our second child was born July 28, 1969; and our third child was born October 7, 1970. So our marriage was sealed in the temple for time and all eternity, and our children were born under the covenant. What a *blessing*!

Life is not easy. There are many trials and mountains with tribulation to climb. When we have sometimes gotten off the path of righteousness, it is necessary to have faith and trust in our Savior. Repent, having a broken heart and a contrite spirit. Keep the commandments that our heavenly Father and Jesus Christ has given us. Follow the will of our heavenly Father and not our will. It is so worth earning our salvation with hope of exaltation. Because of the Atonement of our Savior, this is possible.

Now I understand why when I drove past the temple in Salt Lake City during the time I was singing professionally, I felt the Spirit so strongly, and I didn't understand why back then. And when I first laid my eyes on Roy Horsley, I felt the same Spirit that, at the time, I didn't understand. My love and friendship with my Savior all my life caused me to be blessed to have the feelings I had. Also, I was directed to turn my back on my singing career when I was (after seven years) finally beginning to climb the path to fame. I knew I would never make a success of my marriage if I continued to travel constantly as I did. Roy and our marriage were more important to me than all the fame and fortune in the world. I was given an opportunity to go through the rest of my life with my husband if I lived worthy of that blessing.

CHAPTER 11

Randal Lynn Horsley

It was written in my medical history that I would never have a child when Roy and I were first married. I had severe pain and was taken to the doctor. I was given an exploratory surgery. The doctor thought I had a tubal pregnancy and learned that it was a large ovarian cyst. During the surgery, he also saw the condition of my womb, etc. He told me I would never be able to have children. I was devastated.

I would not believe I could not have children. I fasted over and over again, exercising all the faith and trust in my Savior. I would not allow myself to believe children would not come to me.

An infertility specialist came to Ely, which was close to where we were living. I made an appointment to see this doctor. He instructed me with the things I must do and then put me on a temperature chart. That would tell me if I, in fact, was pregnant. When the chart said I was pregnant, the doctor began progesterone injections. They were given to me for a three-month period.

During my fifth month of pregnancy, I came down with toxemia. I was hospitalized. I was in a large room with other women that were hospitalized. The woman next to my bed was on oxygen. A visitor came to see her and was smoking in the room. The nurse came in and sent the visitor out immediately. The nurse came over, opened the window, which was located next to my bed, in order to get the smoke out of the room as quickly as possible. It was Christmastime and very cold, with a wind coming through the window, and I acquired pneumonia on top of having toxemia. I came down with an extremely high temperature. I was packed with ice from my head to my feet because of the fever. Roy was telephoned because he was working in Hawthorne, Nevada, due to a strike at Kennecott Copper where he normally worked. He was contacted by the local police to give him a message that I wasn't expected to live, and Roy was escorted out of town until he could be on his way to Ely where I was hospitalized.

 I had in my thoughts that if I could somehow learn to relax, even though I was having excruciating chills, when time came for my delivery, it would be easier for my baby and for me. I tried so hard to relax. As soon as I did, my baby kicked me so hard that it put me right back into the excruciating chills. I was given a priesthood blessing. I didn't die. However, I was put on total bed rest for the remainder of my pregnancy. My mother came from Oklahoma to Nevada to be with me until my baby was born.

 The due date was March first. Nothing happened. My baby was born April fourth. People could say the doctor was wrong, saying the due date was March first. I had to have a cesarean section when my baby was delivered. He weighed eight pounds and two and a half ounces. I was in labor from noon one day through the night until noon the next day. The doctor was William B. Ririe. He turned the pregnancy over to Dr. Kendal Jones, and he immediately gave me the cesarean. Dr. Jones told me that another five minutes and my baby and I would not have survived. I was given a spinal block, so I was awake when my baby was born. The doctor who assisted Dr. Jones held my baby up so I could see him. I watched my baby look to the left of the delivery room as if he were taking in everyone that was working there. Then he looked at me. He stared at me for a few minutes and then continued to look to the right of the room. He was born a month later than expected, and nobody had to support his head for him to look around as he did. Yes, I know he was a ten-month-old baby.

 I had to be in bed at the hospital with my head on my pillow for several hours. I don't recall just how long before I could get up, and in those days, it was mandatory to avoid excruciating headaches after a spinal block. I do remember it was five days before I could be released from the hospital after a C-section. I went to church the Sunday after my baby was born. The bishop came up to me after the service was over. He said to me, "Rozena, I couldn't help but watch you all through sacrament meeting. You held your baby and looked at him all through the meeting."

I remember that I looked at him that long. I was saying a prayer all through the meeting to heavenly Father and my Savior to thank them for sending this child to me. I asked them for help to raise my baby so he will stay close to them and strive to earn eternal life. I prayed with all the faith and trust I could possibly have to know my prayer would be answered. To this day, I have no doubt that my prayer of that day would be answered. It has taken me years to learn not to be overzealous. Randal and I have become close friends, and believe me, I am grateful for being able to accept his free agency that heavenly Father and our Savior has given Randal from the beginning of his life. It's me that has concern for my own actions that I will always strive for eternal life.

When Randal was a toddler, we lived at Sunnyside, Nevada, Wayne E. Kirch Wildlife Management Area. We had no television or telephone other than the radio system that connected us with the office in Ely or Reno as well as the working trucks used in our remote location that could communicate to the regional office. I had so much time to spend with Randal. He was one year of age when we moved there, and I began teaching him his alphabet, to tie his shoes, and later, even to work jigsaw puzzles at his age of two. He loved to help me with my housework. He dried dishes, helped dust, learned to make his own bed and keep his toys picked up. There was a hook at his level so he could keep his coat hung up, and he never threw his clothes around on the floor. He knew where to put his dirty clothes and hung his clean clothes on hooks in his closet. When his baby brother, Ray, was born, Randal loved to help put lotion and powder on Ray after his bath. He was so loving to his little brother. When Ray was a baby, I never had to scold Randal once for hurting him in any way.

Once when Randal and I were in Ely at the J.C. Penny store, Randal's shoelace came undone. He was about two years of age. He sat down on the floor and tied his own shoe. A woman saw him do this and asked me if it would be okay if she untied his shoe and wanted people in the store to come and watch him tie his own shoe. They were amazed as they watched.

I taught lessons to primary children in Lund, Nevada, when we lived at Sunnyside. I was preparing lunch for Randal before I drove to Lund to teach a lesson. Randal had been playing in the yard that had a nice chain-link fence around it. I called Randal to come in to eat lunch. He didn't come. I went outside and walked around the house to find him. He wasn't there. I called out as loud as I could… there was no Randal. I called Roy to let him know Randal was missing. Roy came home. It wasn't long before everyone at Sunnyside searched for him.

We found that the neighbor's two children, one little boy, Tim, who was Randal's age of four, and his little sister, Jessica, of age three, were missing. It had been noon when I was aware of Randal being gone. The hours had grown to early evening when the children showed up, coming down a mountain. Randal and Timmy were on each side of a big deer shed they had found, carrying it home. Jessica was trying to keep up with the boys. When I saw Randal, I couldn't scold him. Instead, I put my arms around him, held him close to me, and cried. I thanked heavenly Father for the children being safely home. Mountain lions were known to be in our area. It was cold enough that the temperatures were extremely cold in the mountains. It was such a blessing the children were fine.

When Randal was three years old, we were in Dallas, Texas, visiting a friend, La Verne. She took care of Ray (he was a baby), and we took Randal to Six Flags over Texas. As we were entering the gate of Six Flags, he ran a little ahead of us and turned around and said, "Oh, this is the best day of my life." What a precious memory!

When Randal was five years of age, I became sick. He came up to me and took me by the hand and guided me to the living room couch. He had me lay down. He put a pillow under my head and said, "Mommy, don't worry, I will take care of you. He went to the kitchen, got a stool to stand on, and fixed me a peanut butter sandwich."

Another memory: One day, Randal came up to me and told me he learned a new song in primary. (Primary is a children's program in the Church of Jesus Christ of Latter-Day Saints.) He told me he loved the song. I ask him to sing it to me. The words were:

> Whenever I hear the song of a bird
> Or look at the blue, blue sky.
> Whenever I feel the rain on my face
> Or the wind as it rushes by.
> Whenever I touch a velvet rose
> Or walk by our lilac tree,
> I'm glad that I live in this beautiful world
> Heavenly Father created for me.
>
> He gave me my eyes that I might see
> The color of butterfly wings.
> He gave me my ears that I might hear
> The magical sound of things.
> He gave me my life, my mind, my heart.
> I thank him reverently
> For all his creations, of which I'm a part.
> Yes, I know Heavenly Father loves me.

My mother sent me a small book explaining reflexology when our sons were young. It has pictures of how and where to rub feet to remove their crystals to help them feel better if they are ill. When colds, flu, or other illness came along, I told them I would rub the crystals in their feet so they would feel better. One day, Randal was not feeling well, and he came up to me and said, "Mommy, would you rub the 'diamonds' out of my feet?"

Randal came to the house after a hunting trip at the Overton Wildlife Management Area. He was barely old enough to hunt. He got home from his hunt. He still had his jacket on.

He was holding a mallard duck in one hand and his gun in the other. He said, "Mom, look at my first mallard." Then he said, "Dad, will you come out and clean my duck for me?"

Dad said, "Son, if you're old enough to kill a duck, you're old enough to clean the duck. Let's go out, and I'll teach you how to clean it."

Randal brought his cleaned duck to the kitchen. I said, "Randal, is it okay if I cook your duck for our dinner? I haven't thawed anything out for tonight."

Randal replied, "Mom, if I'm old enough to shoot a duck, and I'm old enough to clean the duck, I'm old enough to cook the duck. Will you show me what to do and I'll do it?"

I ask Randal to wash his hands good, rinse the duck, and put the duck in cold, salted water to soak it. Then I showed him how to season it and then cook it. He did a good job.

When Randal was around twelve years of age, he walked up to me and said, "Mom, I fear for your salvation."

I replied, "What are you talking about?"

He answered, "I've noticed you. When you are with someone you really like and respect, you are so nice to them, and it's obvious you like them. Until you have that same attitude with the fellow standing on the street with long hair, wearing an earring, and no shoes, I fear for your salvation."

That comment from my twelve-year-old son has never left my mind. I have tried to show care for everyone, and I know that's the way my Savior wants me to be.

Randal and Ray both have been boys that as they grew up, they always took care of the smaller children in their life that were being a "bullied." They would defend them on the school bus, at school, or other places.

Randal and Ray both learned to ride horses, work with machinery, fish, and hunt; participate in 4-H and scouts; play T-ball, basketball, and football; and play the piano, guitar, and trumpet. Randal earned the Louis Armstrong Satchmo Award. Wikipedia explains this as a "Top Senior Jazz Award," The highest-level interscholastic award given to students at high school. Randal's honor remains on the wall of the Moapa Valley High School.

Randal was the president of his freshman class in high school. When he was a sophomore, he was captain of his football team. The first game out, Overton went to Kanab, Utah (a team with players older and bigger than Overton's team). Randal was injured during that game, which broke his arm in three different places. That put him out of football for the rest of the year.

When Randal was a freshman in high school, he came to me and told me he wanted to wrestle in school. (I was not familiar with high school wrestling.) They didn't have that program years ago in Oklahoma when I was in school. I had only seen wrestling on television and didn't forget about "Gorgeous George." So I told Randal no. I didn't want him to wrestle. As a senior in high school, the wrestling coach approached Randal and told him he wanted him to wrestle. That he really believed if he worked hard, he could make it to State. Randal had to lose some weight. He didn't have the right gear to wear to help him lose the weight, so he wrapped himself in large plastic bags, ran up, and down a hill, lifted weights, and anything he could do to get in shape for wrestling. He worked so hard to accomplish what he needed to do. Randal did wrestle only that one year and took third in State. I have always regretted to have discouraged him when he was a freshman.

Randal served a two-year mission for the Church of Jesus Christ of Latter-Day Saints in the Canada Winnipeg Mission. While there, Elder Horsley taught seminary students at "Carry the Kettle Indian Reservation" as well as taught the children "beginning piano lessons." Carry the Kettle Reservation had been closed for years for missionaries to serve the Assiniboine Indians. Elder Horsley and Elder Foote, together, were the first missionaries to reopen Carry the Kettle. Elder Horsley had many assignments during his mission. One that was very special was serving as a branch president at Sioux Narrows, Ontario, for the period of time that was needed.

Randal was working on his PhD in medical research at the University of Iowa. Randal became ill with ischemic. He was in the hospital and was to be given a surgery the next morning. The doctors gave him a 50 percent chance for survival. A student friend brought a friend to see Randal the night prior to his surgery. The friend he brought was a palmer chiropractor. The chiropractor asked Randal if he could do an adjustment for him. Randal thought about the fact he had a fifty chance of survival, so he agreed.

The next morning, Randal was taken for an X-ray before the surgery. When seeing the results of the X-ray, they asked Randal, "What did you do during night?" Randal told them he had an adjustment. They said, "Randal, you don't need the surgery. Everything has changed overnight." Randal was weak. However, he was on his feet, and he left the University of Iowa and registered into the Palmer College of Chiropractic in Davenport, Iowa. He was able to test and bypass chemistry and also biochemistry because he had taught both subjects to freshman and sophomore students at the University of Nevada, Las Vegas (UNLV) while working on his master's degree. Randal is the first of our family to earn a college degree. Randal is now a palmer chiropractor and a clinical nutritionist. He opened his own clinic in Delaware. He didn't have help from his parents for finances. He and Susan, Randal's wife, worked hard as Randal got his degrees. Randal continues to get new certifications. He is happy that he has a profession to help others.

Randal met Susan while in Las Vegas. Suzy, as she likes to be called, has her own business—"Residential Housing Appraisal." She began appraising houses as she worked her way to earn her business degree at UNLV. She continued after graduation to appraise homes. Now, they are co-owners of The Wellness Junction and Residential Housing Appraisal. They have been married for twenty-three years.

I was in Iowa visiting Randal and Suzy when he was still in school. Suzy was working upstairs with her appraisal paperwork. I fixed lunch and took it up to her. As I was going downstairs, I was so pleased to hear her say, "Thank you, Mom."

When they had moved to Delaware, once again I was visiting with Randal and Suzy. She had been asked to make some deviled eggs for a party. She was so busy working and asked me if I would make the deviled eggs. I agreed. She had the right paraphernalia to make the deviled eggs. Suzy handed me a recipe for me to follow. Wow! My deviled eggs were beautiful.

Suzy served several years for the young ladies in mutual. She loves to go to camp with the girls. She teaches them many things such as painting, knitting, lessons to learn, and has a great rapport with them, even when they reach an age when they are no longer in her class. Occasionally, her girls still contact her

Yes, Suzy is a perfectionist in everything she does. She is such a hard worker, and working is what she likes to do. However, she truly loves the Atlantic Ocean and enjoys living near that area. Suzy, I love you.

What a blessing it is for Roy and myself to be parents for Randal Lynn Horsley.

He continues to achieve a life filled with new achievements. Currently, he is earning his PPL (Private Pilot License). He is truly very interested in this new adventure.

Randal, I love you, my son.

HE RESTORETH MY SOUL

Dr. Randal L. Horsley
Palmer Chiropractor
Clinical Nutritionist

Owner of "The Wellness Junction"
Millsboro, Delaware

ROZENA CAROLINE HORSLEY

Randal and Susan Horsley

CHAPTER 12

Kevin Paul Horsley

Fifteen months after Randal Lynn Horsley was born, I gave birth to Kevin Paul Horsley. What a treasure. After the C-section with Randal, I was told I would be able to give a natural birth to my baby, Kevin Paul. However, he was breach. Another C-section was necessary. The date was set for July 28, 1969.

When Kevin was born, in the delivery room, Kevin was held up so I could see him. He was such a handsome little son. He had the dark hair like his dad and looked so much like Roy. I never heard him cry. He looked at me and smiled. He was quickly taken from the room. I was taken to my hospital room, and once again, I was to keep my head on my pillow for many hours to avoid having excruciating headaches. As I laid there, Dr. William B. Ririe came into my room to tell me that my baby was not well. He was constantly being treated by the doctors. There I was, laying there with major concern. Dr. Ririe left my room. However, he kept coming back and telling me the doctors were doing all they could do for Kevin.

I will forever recall the many times Dr. Ririe returned. He stood by the window in my room, looking out with concern. After twelve-and-one-half hours, Dr. Ririe came back once more. He told me my baby didn't make it. He was deceased. When Roy came in to me, he told me that he had remained in the waiting room until he was told that the doctors had done all they could do, and they knew Kevin would not survive. Roy, along with Uncle Bud Hendrix, went to

Kevin and placed their hands on his head and gave him a priesthood name and a blessing. Immediately after the blessing was given, Kevin looked up at his dad, smiled, and died. He had come to this earth to receive a body and a name and a blessing.

There I was, alone, in my bed, being told I could not take my head off my pillow. Roy came into my room and told me that a graveyard service had been planned, and Kevin would be buried that day. I would not be able to attend because of doctor's orders that I was to stay in bed with my head on my pillow. I immediately got up. I was going to my baby's burial. Nobody in this world would stop me from being there. I don't recall making the trip from Ely, Nevada, to the Lund Cemetery, where our baby was buried. The next memory I have was standing over the grave that had been dug, and Kevin had been placed in his little casket. Roy was holding me up. I had the excruciating headache. My incision felt as though it would open up right there. My heartache was unbearable.

I saw Roy's Dad standing on the other side of the grave, holding our son, Randal. Randal was fifteen months of age. He was looking at Kevin's casket with great concern on his little face. We watched as Keven Paul Horsley was lowered into the ground. The next thing I recall was being taken to Harold Lynn and Lois Horsley's (home **of** Roy's parents in Lund) and put to bed. The pain I felt was unbearable. Spiritually, physically, and impossible to deal with. I truly wanted to die. Then, I thought about my son, Randal. I must live. I had to be here for my son. Then, I thought of Roy. He needed me to help raise Randal. "I must be strong," I told myself. My mother-in-law, Lois Horsley, took excellent care of me.

She kept me clean, fed me, and most importantly, cared for Randal. I don't remember how many days I was in that bed. I had an appointment to go to my doctor for a checkup. I was taken to the room where the doctor would see me. When the doctor walked in, I broke down and cried and cried and cried. I was placed on the bed in the room and continued to cry. The doctor just closed the door and gave me the time I needed to cry. I was taken back to Lund and placed, once again, in bed. Again, I don't remember how long I was there.

Finally, I gained strength to think about needing to go to Ely, shop for groceries, and go to my home, which was at Sunnyside, Nevada. We lived on a Wildlife Management Area. I drove myself to Ely and went to the grocery store, got a cart, and filled it with groceries. A friend saw me there and came up to talk with me. She said, "Oh, I see you have had your baby. Did you have a boy or a girl?" I could not say one word to her. I quickly left my cart filled with groceries and ran from the store, got into my car, and once again, I cried and cried and cried. Finally, I was able to drive back to Lund. Randal and I returned to Sunnyside.

Days went by. I had many baby clothes that had been gifts from a shower that was given for our new son. I looked at everything and got the gifts together to be given away. Oh, how difficult it was. There were more tears.

Thank goodness I had Randal. He was such a sweet little boy. He needed me. I needed him. Roy was a wonderful husband and Dad. He was such a blessing to us both.

Never had I imagined that life could be so difficult. Oh, how I wanted my baby. And that feeling went on for years. Through prayer, faith in my Savior, and study of the scriptures, I found strength. One day, the thoughts came to me that Kevin Paul Horsley was such a special spirit that he didn't have to go through trials and temptations on this earth. He was already in the celestial kingdom of heaven. It was not up to me to walk beside him and teach him the importance of living righteously to gain eternal life. It was up to me to live worthy of such blessings and, once again, be with Kevin Paul and to teach Randal the importance that he, too, would have such a blessing.

It has been in my heart and soul to live worthy that someday, when our Savior returns to earth and Kevin will be resurrected and will return to his infant body, I will be resurrected as well. Kevin will be placed in my arms. Roy and I will raise him to adulthood during the millennium, when Satan will be bound for 1,000 years, and we can walk with Jesus Christ here on this earth. I have dedicated my mind and my heart to be worthy for that time. This has been the greatest blessing I have been given to have such a remarkable knowledge that has dedicated my heart and soul to do my best.

I shall never forget a very vivid dream I had about Kevin. One that will live with me forever. I was holding my baby. He put his little arm around my neck and patted me on my shoulder to express his love for me. Never have I felt love so deeply through that dream. Expressing that love in this story helps me to feel the blessing that is mine. Kevin knows of the love I have for him. I thank my heavenly Father for my children.

CHAPTER 13

Ray Allen Horsley

After Kevin Paul Horsley died. I thought I never wanted another child. I couldn't possibly experience the heartache again. However, I thought about raising Randal Lynn Horsley as an only child. I prayed about it with fasting. I knew I was to have another child.

Again, fifteen months went by, and I delivered another son, Ray Allen Horsley. It was my third C-section. In the delivery room, I heard the words once again, "It's a boy!"

I said, "I don't care if it's a boy or a girl…is he okay?"

The doctor lifted up Ray so I could see him. Ray was screaming to the top of his lungs. The doctor said, "Could he be anything but okay?"

I thought Ray was handsome and wonderful. My three sons… Randal had the color of auburn hair, Kevin, brunette like his dad, and Ray was blonde. Each of them had the same features. They were such handsome babies.

I certainly wanted to keep my head on the pillow as long as I was told, following the spinal block. I didn't want the excruciating headaches again. When they brought Ray in to me, I was so grateful to have him close to me and in my arms. I didn't take my eyes off him for a second. I was always sad when the nurse took him back to the nursery.

When the hospital stay was over, we went to Roy's parents' house in Lund. As Roy and I walked in to the house, Randal was sitting on the countertop, watching his Grandma Lois washing dishes. Grandma Lois lifted Randal down from the countertop. Grandma and Randal were so excited to see Ray for the first time. There was so much love that filled that room for Ray from his loved ones.

When we arrived home at Sunnyside, it was such a joy to take care of Ray. To feed him, give him his baths, hold him, and have "rocking chair time" that made memories to last forever. Randal watched me give Ray his baths. After each bath, Randal helped me gently rub lotion on Ray and helped to powder him. He wanted to help put a blanket on him to keep him warm. Never once did I have to scold Randal for being mean to Ray. I love Randal and Ray so much.

As Ray grew, I tried to do as I had done with Randal. I held him in my lap to teach him as I did Randal so he would learn his alphabet, tie his shoe very early in life, etc. I learned very early that Ray would rather be on the floor playing with toys. There was no changing his mind. To my astonishment, he did learn very early in his life. He watched Randal and learned in his own way and time. They both loved to play with tinker toys and built some astonishing items.

It was so great to see the boys growing up together. At Sunnyside, we went out together as a family and enjoyed the mountains and the beautiful place where we lived. We even went out to watch a new highway being built, which went from Sunnyside to Hiko, Nevada. Until that time, the paved road ended at our home, and it was a dirt road that was like a roller coaster to make the trip to Hiko. The boys loved their dad to give them an exciting ride…going up and down faster than I ever wanted. However, I enjoyed seeing the excitement the boys had.

Ray was only two years of age when Roy was transferred from Wayne E. Kirch Wildlife Management Area (Sunnyside) to Key Pittman Wildlife Management Area (Hiko). Roy was the manager at Hiko. We were only there one year when Roy was transferred to Overton Wildlife Manager (Overton, Nevada). Ray enjoyed fishing, hunting, and the joys that come from that kind of life. Ray, as well as Randal, were taught to operate tractors, back hoes, and other machinery. There was always a lot of work to be done, and they learned to work.

When we lived at Hiko, we attended church at Alamo, Nevada. I had a job conducting the music for the opening exercise in Sunday school. Roy would sit with the congregation and Randal and Ray. As I was coming off the stage one Sunday, Ray had disappeared. At the time, he was only two, and I was concerned. I looked for him and wasn't having much luck. I began to open the door to different age groups as they were in class. I opened a door to a class of older children. There was Ray. I apologized to the teacher and ask Ray to come with me. The teacher said, "Ray is fine. Please let him stay. He answers questions as well as all the children, and we want him to be here with us." Yes, Ray was always his own person.

He disappeared once when we were in Las Vegas at the mall. It was Christmastime. Now, that was *really scary*. We found him on the front row of a big display where the Christmas music was playing, and the characters were moving around. Ray was having a wonderful time enjoying all that was being performed.

One Mother's Day, Ray excused himself after we ate lunch. He asked for a needle and thread. He went into his bedroom, shut, and locked the door. He was in his room for hours. I knocked on the door and asked if he was okay. He answered "Yes." It seemed liked forever before he came out. He handed me a square piece of material. He had cut smaller denim squares and sewed them by hand together, then sewed the small squares to the big denim background, cut out a large red heart which he sewed to the denim, and had written on it "I Love You." He made it as a Mother's Day gift. I have kept it in my piano bench. It has been with me for many years. His little fingers were pricked from sewing.

He came to the door of our home in Overton when he was a little boy. I was in the kitchen preparing a meal. He knocked on the door. I opened the door, and there was my little boy, Ray, with a bouquet of wild roses he had picked for me. He was holding them behind his back. He held the flowers in front of him and handed them to me and said, "I love you, Mom." He continued each year to bring me flowers. These are memories that I treasure.

Ray and Randal learned to play the piano, trumpet, and guitar. They could both sing so well. They liked to sing together as they each played their guitars. They were not interested in performing for others…just our family. Ray played first trumpet in the high school band before he was even in high school. He also played in the high school jazz band. He not only played exceptionally well, but he also had such a stage presence too. It was a thrill to see and hear his talent as he performed.

Randal and Ray both enjoyed sports. They played T-ball, baseball, basketball, and football and took karate lessons. They were both in 4-H with lambs and pigs to raise, care for, exercise, show, and sell their animals. Ray won grand champion for his pig at the Clark County Jr. Livestock Show, sponsored by McDonald's. Ray also won the Pee Wee Showmanship Award. Ronald McDonald handed out the trophies for the different classes. Randal won a belt buckle for his sheep and won the reserve grand champion carcass for his pig. Ray came home and cut some out some small boards and wrapped the boards with aluminum foil to make trophies. He invited his friends to our home and presented them with trophies of their own. He wanted them to share the joy of winning a trophy.

Ray was flown to the hospital in Las Vegas when he was injured playing football. He had injured his spleen. The same year, he played football and made the leading tackles when his team went to State.

When I turned seventy years of age, Ray sent me the most beautiful card and letter that thanked me for being a wonderful mom. When each year passed by and I was growing older, the words lifted me up more than he will ever know.

Ray married young. He worked hard with several jobs to support his wife, RuthAnn. They had a precious daughter, Brittanie, and a son, Cyler. Ray tried out for LVMPD. He was hired after going through the tests only once. Many must retest two or three times to pass the tests before they are hired. He tested for a helicopter pilot position. Came out number one. He retired early in life as a helicopter pilot, search and rescue, instructor for new pilots, etc. He helped RuthAnn with her broker (real estate) business. One week after his retirement, he was called to be bishop for a single's ward in Las Vegas.

After three years, he began flying helicopter tours over the Grand Canyon for a private company. He remains as bishop.

He and RuthAnn have had many events for the single's in parks with good food, games, and fun. They often invite the young people to come to their home for meetings, dinners, etc.

Ray and RuthAnn have been so good to us. They have taken us to Arcadia, California to the Santa Anita Park to experience the horse races, the Dodgers baseball game (even bought us some peanuts and cracker jacks at the game), and the Ruby Princess Cruise to Mexico—so many five-star restaurants. They have opened their door to us to stay with them in their home for a long period of time when Roy was diagnosed with cancer. Radiation and chemotherapy were necessary treatments. Randal and Suzy have paid our flights to Delaware multiple times.

Dr. Randal Horsley corresponded with the oncologist and radiologist and provided and sent his dad with holistic supplements that made the suffering not as painful and a better possibility for a cancer-free diagnosis. Fact is, Roy is now cancer-free. All he has to do now is testing every six months, to be sure it doesn't return. Roy and I are so blessed, our children are so kind and loving to us. Randal and Suzy had taken us to skeet shooting competitions, to the Atlantic Ocean barbecues, we have enjoyed traveling, eating at fabulous places with them. He recently took his dad on history sites in Pennsylvania. They have traveled from Delaware to Nevada many times. Miles between Nevada and Delaware cannot keep us from being together for Christmas, birthdays, or no special occasions. It's called love!. Our children gave us memories to last forever for our 50th Anniversary. Flowers, pictures, delicious food, invitations for friends and family, they did not miss a thing. I'm certain it had to be the best 50th party ever given in our hometown of Lund.

RuthAnn has been such a good friend for me. I have called her several times to ask for help in one way or another. She is so knowledgeable about so many things and is always willing to do things to help me. We play scrabble together. She beats me 98 percent of the games we play. Once in a while… I win. That's only when I draw the best tiles, which is rare. I still use my knowledge (as amateur as it is) about reflexology to rub RuthAnn's feet. I also rub Roy's, Randal's, and Suzy's feet. When Randal and I are together, Randal rubs my feet too. Ray's feet must be ticklish because he won't allow me to rub his feet. When he was my little boy, he allowed me to rub his feet anytime he wasn't feeling well. Talking about rubbing feet, Roy, Randal, Suzy, and RuthAnn enjoy getting their feet rubbed. It makes me feel it is a way of expressing my love for them.

Ray and RuthAnn are the grandparents of four children. Their daughter, Brittanie, and her husband, Robby, have three children: Berkley (age eight), Baylor (age seven), and Bostyn (age three in December of 2021). Their son, Cyler, and his wife, Eve, have one son: Killian (age six). The grandchildren are talented as well as being very beautiful and handsome.

I thank Heavenly Father each day and night for our precious family. And even though I am not their mom, I feel that RuthAnn and Suzy are my daughters. For special times, I always pick out a card for each of them that has the right words to say. However, *never* do I pick out a daughter-in-law card. In my heart, I am their mom, and even though I didn't give birth to them, I love them as my own.

A few years ago, Ray went into a store in Las Vegas and saw a beautiful gift that he bought for me. It was a woman dressed in white, holding a baby dressed in white. The mother is sitting on a seat, and the baby is standing on her lap, with her hands holding him up as they look at each other. Ray had written a note and placed it in my gift. He wrote, "This caused me to wonder how it will be when you have the blessing of, once again, being with Kevin." This gift has been placed on a single glass shelf, and there are white flowers of roses and daisies. It is on a wall in our living room. It is a gift that I will cherish forever.

Ray, I am so thankful that I prayed (with fasting) that I would be blessed to have another baby when I was so concerned about the experiences I had when Kevin Paul died. I would not have been able to have another child because of medical reasons. I believe you were a miracle, sent to us from heaven.

"I love you, my son."

HE RESTORETH MY SOUL

Ray A. Horsley
Police Officer
Pilot

Ray and RuthAnn Horsley

Horsleys in Hawaii
Ray and RuthAnn
Randal and Susan

Robby and Brittanie
(Horsley) Reid

HE RESTORETH MY SOUL

Berkley Reid

Baylor Reid

HE RESTORETH MY SOUL

Bostyn Reid

Cyler and Eve Horsley

HE RESTORETH MY SOUL

Killian Horsley

CHAPTER 14

JANET

Janet is the daughter of Carlton Lee Rice and Cora Martha (Jaggars) Rice. Cora Martha has been known as "Mickie." Both parents of Janet are deceased.

Mickie and I were both born in the year 1940. She is my half aunt. We were close and kept in touch with each other through the years. Mickie was so close to Jesus Christ and had concern for others. She did what she could to help others in need and always prayed for them. I had deep love for Mickie and certainly miss her. She was deceased 2015.

Carlton Lee Rice has been deceased since 1976. Carlton and Mickie visited with me when I was singing at the Spinosa Supper Club in Baton Rouge, Louisiana. It was such a surprise that they traveled from Oklahoma to Louisiana just to see me. I was on tour at the time being, booked through Music Corporation of America. Very seldom did I see people I knew (especially my loved ones). It meant so much to me.

Janet is their only child. She is married to Jeffrey Chapman. They wanted children. However, that hasn't happened.

When Mickie died, Janet contacted me to inform me of her death. Since that time, Janet and I have been so close that we have a telephone contact almost each day. I have learned to love Janet as though she is my daughter. We had to have known each other in the preexistence. I truly believe she has more faith and trust in Jesus

Christ, even more than her mother did. She, too, loves people, and when she knows they have need, she helps them in whatever way she can.

Janet has had physical problems and a wheelchair is needed for her needs. Yet she has a beautiful attitude and enjoys watching birds, squirrels, good movies, and other television shows of interest. She is knowledgeable about so many things. It is certainly enjoyable to talk with Janet. She gives me a lift when I am not feeling well. She lets me know she is praying for me. Janet has been such a blessing for me and my husband. Janet and Jeff have added "sunshine" to our life.

This book just wouldn't be complete without mentioning the Chapmans.

Janet and Jeff, it is my prayer that you will have the blessings of heavenly Father and Jesus Christ always.

CHAPTER 15

SEVENTEEN YEARS IN LUND, NEVADA (SO FAR)

Prior to moving to Lund, I worked at Overton substation for Las Vegas Metropolitan Police Department. Overton is sixty-five miles from Las Vegas. I worked with one sergeant and seven officers. My job was to take crime reports, register handguns, take fingerprints for noncriminals, prepare monthly reports, etc. There were mandatory seminars for training. I served the residence of Moapa Valley and LVMPD for eleven years, full time, and four years prior as part-time, so a total of fifteen years.

Other jobs prior to the substation: Wayne Newton Aramis Arabians (secretary), Dr. Lance Robertson (receptionist), Owned a Bird Store in Las Vegas (R Birds), Kennecott Copper Corporation (stenographer); I owned an exercise business (Rozena's Slenderella Salon) in Ely, which I sold before we moved to Sunnyside, Nevada; and as previously mentioned, for seven years, I sang professionally. I was booked through Music Corporation of America.

Roy and I were called as missionaries for the Addiction Recovery Program. During the years we attended, we had a yearly training which was held in Sparks, Carson City, and Elko, Nevada. We learned so many things as we taught the lessons to those who attended. One lesson was that we should repent, immediately, whenever we are upset (for reasons we caused) and also for reasons someone else caused. Sometimes Roy and I have a disagreement. Now, we handle our problems in that way. We learned that when we become upset or angry, the Holy Ghost will leave us. The Holy Ghost will not return until we apologize and repent with a broken heart and a contrite spirit. We need the Holy Ghost to guide us and to give peace to our heart and mind.

This lesson is very humbling, and it certainly works. Disagreements between us have almost disappeared. We are becoming "one" with each other. Another lesson was the importance of doing God's will and not rationalize to do our will. In other words, "keep the commandments." There were many more lessons that has helped us live with happiness. It was such a joy to witness some that attended the classes truly turned their life around for the positive. Their countenance actually changed for the good. There were many that didn't change their addiction habits. At least we know the spirit planted some seeds within their hearts. Someday, they may have desire to acknowledge what they must do and repent and receive forgiveness from our Savior. The atonement happened for everyone that truly repents with a broken heart and a contrite spirit.

Roy and I have been happy for different callings in the church. We are so blessed to live in this little community of Lund, Nevada. We have opportunity to give and receive service from others. So many people set such a good example for us, and we try our best to always set as good examples for others. Our testimony of the restored gospel of truth and righteousness grows as we attend the Church of Jesus Christ of Latter-Day Saints. We recognize that our testimonies are under construction, and we learn more each day of pleasing our heavenly Father and Jesus Christ, our Savior, and live each day to have the Holy Ghost to comfort us and guide us.

I have learned when I suffer from physical pain, hurt with a broken heart, disappointment, or in any other way, I know that Jesus Christ suffered more than anyone on this earth when He atoned for our sins. Jesus knows that we go through pain and trials so we can grow spiritually. Any time we fear, it is important to get rid of that fear and replace the fear with faith and trust in Jesus Christ. It works when we "keep the commandments" and do God's will, and not our will.

We partake of the sacrament each Sunday as we attend church. We must be worthy of partaking of the sacrament. Each week, we are to remember to live righteously. If we stumble and sin, we are to feel sorry for our wrong. Sincerely repent and become worthy of partaking of the sacrament again. Heavenly Father is pleased when we pray often and always remember His beloved Son, Jesus Christ and the atonement. We will have a blessing from heaven to have the Spirit of our Savior with us always.

"Eternal life" is the best blessing we can ever have. It is necessary to go through the grace of Jesus Christ to earn eternal life. We do that by following Him. Eternal life is the best blessing we can have. The scriptures teach us that heavenly Father and Jesus Christ are so willing to forgive us when we sin and repent with a broken heart and contrite spirit. I know that is true. With my experiences in life, I have felt peace within my soul when I have had a broken heart and contrite spirit and repented of my sins. I have felt the love from heavenly Father and Jesus Christ. The feeling of their love has penetrated every pour of my body. When I have stumbled once more, I have gone through the same experience. The forgiveness always helps me once again.

The two greatest commandments:

1. Love the Lord, our God, with all our might, mind, and strength.
2. Love our neighbor as our self. (Yes, we must love our self.)

The way we show our love to heavenly Father and Jesus Christ is to keep the commandments. heavenly Father and Jesus Christ are as one. We must be as one with them. Heavenly Father loves each one of His children. I am a child of God. You are a child of God too.

I know that Jesus Christ "restoreth my soul." You, too, can experience the same blessing.

This book was written about the story of my life.

In the name of Jesus Christ.

Amen.

The remainder of my book reminds me of Paul Harvey saying "And now, for the rest of my story."

When I received my DNA at my age of 80, as my story goes, I was devastated to think Henry Paul Eads was not my biological father. Only this morning I received a phone call from a person I asked to study my DNA so I would know for a fact that someone other than my father I grew up with (though deceased) was my biological father. This took quite a while to receive what was learned.

I was told that even though DNA was not taken from my father, mother, nor my only sibling, however, my sister's two daughters have had their DNA taken and my two sons have had their DNA. Studying these DNA's along with my DNA, it appears that my sister, Peggy Jean, is truly my full sister (not my half-sister.) This could be determined by the study of my relatives. This shows that Henry Paul Eads is, in fact, my biological father. I am so grateful that he chose to put his name on my birth certificate.

We are told we can have a professional study our lineage for a fee. We are all a child of God. That is what really matters.

In receiving the news, that Henry Paul Eads is my biological father, I felt a relief that came over me. It also caused me to recall my experiences of my life once again from the time I was born until now.

I am reminded of the "Lord's Prayer" that Jesus Christ taught that appears within the Bible.

Matthew 6:9–13

And after this manner therefore pray ye:

Our Father which art in heaven.
Hallowed be thy name.
Thy kingdom come, Thy will be done in earth as it is in heaven.

Give us this day our daily bread
And forgive us our debts, as we forgive our debtors
And lead us not into temptation
But deliver us from evil;
For thine is the kingdom, and the power,
and the glory for ever. Amen

(We are taught to do our Father's will and not OUR will.
And to forgive us as we forgive others.)

Oh how important to acknowledge that which we should do. The things that will keep us on the path that will lead us back to our Father in heaven.

"He Restoreth My Soul." Speaking of Jesus Christ who leads and guides us to know those things we must learn to do during our existence on our earth life.

It's obvious my parents had major trials during their life prior to their departures from this earth. Also, my sister had her trials from the time she was two years of age. It's clear to me she was a witness to the extreme contention between mother and daddy. She was taken from daddy when mother took her to Oklahoma to be with her mother during their extremely harsh words, one with another. She knew when I was born, I must have been the reason for all of her heartache. I (100 percent) forgive my sister for all the torment she put me through. I also forgive my parents for any and all the problems they experienced during their lifetime on this earth.

Mother once told me she felt Daddy was having a relationship with another woman during the time they lived in Colorado. It seems to me that she perhaps thought she would get even. Thus, when she went to Oklahoma to leave Daddy and learned she was with child, she, and Daddy both thought I was another man's child. I believe they both died before it was proven, that Henry Paul Eads is, in fact, my biological Father.

As I said in the beginning of my book, I love each of my family with my heart and soul. This statement comes from the depth of my soul.

This book was written about the story of my life.

In the name of Jesus Christ

Amen

Wayne Newton and WN ARASTARZA

Rozena Horsley, Ranch Secretary

Aramus Arabians is located in Logandale, Nevada, about sixty miles north of Las Vegas. As the entire horse operation grows larger every year, so do the facilities. There are presently four barns, including nearly one hundred stalls, and a complete breeding and testing facility, a swimming pool for exercising horses, three training rings, and acres of beautiful green pastures.

For information regarding our stud services or sales list, please write Aramus Arabians. PO Box 248 Logandale, Nevada 89021, or call (702) 397-8091.

<u>Since this information, Wayne Newton's Aramus Arabians has been sold.</u>

Visitors Always Welcome

Maxi, a recently birdnapped prize hyacinth macaw, nuzzles her owner, Rozena Horsley.

Rozena Horsley and Maxi from "R" Birds

Rozena with Blue and Gold "R" Birds

ABOUT THE AUTHOR

Rozena is from Oklahoma. She attended Eastern Oklahoma State College. Rozena signed a five-year contract to sing professionally and was booked through Music Corporation of America. She traveled most of the USA as well as performed at Goose Bay Air Force Base in Labrador. When she sang at the Peabody in Memphis, Elvis Presley invited Rozena to his Graceland home, which is mentioned in her book. Rozena ended her singing career of seven years when she married Roy Horsley. She put marriage a priority over constant traveling. Later in life, she was secretary for Wayne Newton's Aramus Arabians in Logandale, Nevada. Rozena and Roy have been married for fifty-six years. They are the parents of three sons (one deceased) and have two grandchildren and four great-grandchildren.

CPSIA information can be obtained
at www.ICGtesting.com
Printed in the USA
BVHW011812060723
666845BV00015B/600